The Unofficial U.S. Census

To David Aretha, friend,
colleague, and one helluva
book editor.

The Unofficial U.S. Census

Things the Official U.S. Census *Doesn't* Tell You About America

Les Krantz & Chris Smith

Skyhorse Publishing

Produced by: Facts That Matter, Inc.
Editor: David Aretha
Researcher: Marci McGrath
Book Design: Julie Nor
Cover Design: Adam Bozarth

All photos courtesy of Shutterstock.

Skyhorse Publishing books may be purchased in bulk at special discounts for sales promotion, corporate gifts, fund-raising, or educational purposes. Special editions can also be created to specifications. For details, contact the Special Sales Department, Skyhorse Publishing, 307 West 36th Street, 11th Floor, New York, NY 10018 or info@skyhorsepublishing.com.

www.skyhorsepublishing.com

10 9 8 7 6 5 4 3 2 1

Library of Congress Cataloging-in-Publication
Krantz, Les.
The unofficial U.S. census : things the official U.S. census doesn't tell you about America / Les Krantz and Chris Smith.
p. cm.
ISBN 978-1-61608-305-2 (hardcover : alk. paper)
1. National characteristics, American. 2. United States--Civilization. 3. United States--Social life and customs. 4. United States--Social conditions. 5. United States--Miscellanea. 6. United States--Statistics. I. Smith, Chris (Christopher Jerome), 1955- II. Title. III. Title: Unofficial United States census.
E169.12.K727 2011
317.3--dc22

2010046835

Printed in China

Acknowledgments

The authors are grateful to David Aretha, our manuscript editor, who as always provided his authors with much more than just wordsmithing and the usual nitpicky fixes. David came in and took charge, from developing our idea to the 11th-hour needs that provided a readable book that "sings" where we hoped it would.

We were proud to have our book acquired by Skyhorse Publishing, one of the newer and hotter New York houses. Our editor there, Julie Matysik, could not have been more helpful and encouraging. Skyhorse Publisher Tony Lyons provided an outstanding team that included Mark Weinstein, a longtime friend in the book world who made the introductions that paved the way for us to get together.

The book's designer, Julie Nor, made all of us look good—not to mention our book, too.

Thanks to historian and researcher Marci McGrath for her usual keen eye for facts and words that were worth including.

Contents

The "Juicy" Census

If you could sneak a peek at the official 2010 census forms returned to the government by American citizens, you'd learn a few things about them and their families. You'd know whether they rent or own, their ages and relationships, their races, and their telephone numbers.

But you wouldn't know that nearly half of Americans keep photos of a pet in their wallet or cell phone. You wouldn't know that a quarter of Americans ages 18 to 50 have at least one tattoo. With just the official census results, you'd never suspect how many Americans 65 or older play paintball, or that the average video game player is 34 years old.

Because the census form or door-to-door census taker didn't ask about those things, the official U.S. Census report will help you count Americans but it won't give you much insight into who they really are. That's where this book comes in. How can you learn the juicy details about American life? Fortunately, people rarely hesitate to answer questions from pollsters and other researchers.

The Unofficial U.S. Census uses a wide variety of sources to answer the questions the government neglected to ask—such things as who we sleep with, what we ingest, what we own, what we drive, how often we have sex, and more.

This unofficial portrait of America draws from surveys by Pew, Gallup, Harris, and other respected polling firms, and from in-depth research by such organizations as the Kinsey Institute and the National Endowment for the Arts. It includes glimpses into the minds of Internet users through such sources as Google data and celebrity-watching websites. And it relies on a staggering volume of government research, from sources including the Bureau of Labor Statistics, FBI, CDC, and even some statistics gathered by the U.S. Census Bureau workers while they are waiting for the next census to come around every 10 years.

In these pages, you'll find out how much credit card debit American households live with, and you'll discover the scary truth about whether the average home has more people or more televisions. You'll learn why 3.5 million commuters have to get a really, really early start to get to work on time.

Although this portrait of America is drawn from mostly serious sources, you are allowed to have fun as you consider the amazing creativity and energy of your fellow citizens. Who knows? By the end of this book, you may think of your neighbors in an entirely new way.

Let the Good Times Roll

How Americans Live and Play

Tattooed Nation

Among many cultural changes in America since the 1930s, one of the easiest to see—literally—is the wider acceptance of tattooing. In 1936, *Life* magazine found that 6% of Americans had at least one tattoo. By 2003, that number had quadrupled among adults 50 and under. How did tattoos go from a few pictures of anchors and tributes to *Mom* on the arms of sailors and bikers to a common fashion accessory for movie stars, rock stars, and even the kid next door?

America: Tattoo Capital of the World

Statistics on the tattoo-culture website Vanishingtattoo.com include:

- With 21,000 tattoo parlors in the U.S., Americans are the most tattooed people on earth.
- According to the American Academy of Dermatologists, a quarter of all Americans from 18 to 50 now have at least one tattoo.
- Among those ages 25 to 29, more than a third are tattooed.
- For people in their 30s, the rate was only slightly lower (28%).

- Nearly as many women (15%) as men (16%) have tattoos.
- According to the men's magazine *FHM,* more than half of the top 50 "sexiest women" have at least one tattoo.

Ink Styles of the Rich and Famous

The popularity of tattoos surged in the 1990s and shows no signs of stopping. Why? A reaction against the more conservative values of parents? Safer tattoo equipment and more colorful ink? Media coverage of talented tattoo artists? All may play a role, but don't underestimate the power of celebrity example.

Many people now get tattoos because it's the hip thing to do. Their "role models," ranging from Britney Spears and Paris Hilton to The Rock, Eminem, and 50 Cent, boast tattoos. Megan Fox, best known for her role in the *Transformers* movies, told an interviewer that she has eight tattoos, at least two of which are visible in red-carpet appearance photos of the actress. Whatever the motivation, tattoos have become a part of the style of America's youth culture in the 21st century.

Vanishingtattoo.com tracks the ink styles of the rich and famous, including the big names below.

Angelina Jolie: Among her many: an Asian tiger on her back, the Roman numeral XIII, a lowercase *h* for her brother James Haven, a Latin cross, the words *Know your rights,* a dragon, and the letter *M* in honor of her late mother, Marcheline.

Brad Pitt: A Khmer-language tattoo of Angelina Jolie's birthday and—get ready—an image of Otzi the Iceman, Europe's famous mummified human.

LeBron James: *CHOSEN* is inked on his back. The NBA star also has a lion head, *The Beast,* his hometown area code (330), a portrait of his son, his mother's name (Gloria), and many others.

Drew Barrymore: A bouquet of flowers on her hip, a butterfly on her stomach, a crescent moon on one of her toes, a fancy cross surrounded by vines, and two angels (with her mother's name and an ex-boyfriend's name beneath them).

Britney Spears: Kabbalah symbols on her neck, a fairy, a daisy circling on one toe, a butterfly, a flower, a star on one hand, lips, and a multicolored cross.

Robert Downey Jr.: The name *Suzie* and a superhero-styled image of himself on his left arm.

Slathered in Ink

Anyone who has watched an NBA game in recent years knows that professional basketball players are "inked" at a much higher rate than the general population. According to the book *In the Paint: Tattoos of the NBA and the Stories Behind Them,* more than 70% of NBA players have a tattoo or two, or sometimes 20. J. R. Smith's arms are nearly covered in tattoos.

In today's Western world, tattoos are widely accepted—at least small ones below the neck. It is not uncommon for a mother and her daughter to get their first tattoos together. *Tattoo* is one of the most searched keywords on the Internet, and the Vanishing Tattoo website claims to have received more than 475 million hits.

As more people get tattoos, more want to remove a tattoo, especially if it features the name of a former lover. But tattoo removal can be painful and costly. Actor Johnny Depp reportedly had only two letters, *na,* removed from his *Winona Forever* tattoo (as in his former girlfriend, actress Winona Ryder). That creative editing leaves him adorned with the amusing motto *Wino Forever.*

Of the 45 million Americans estimated by the Food and Drug Administration to have tattoos, Harris polls have found that 17%

suffer from tattoo regret. A removal process often costs about $40 per square inch of ink removed, although it may take several treatments to complete the process.

Dr. Will Kirby, a tattoo removal expert, told the *Los Angeles Times* in 2009 that about 85% of his clientele were women between 18 and 44 who made at least $50,000 a year. The laser he uses to remove tattoos is most effective on black ink. Yellow and green ink are more difficult to get rid of. And no matter what color the tattoo, the biggest drawback of removal, Dr. Kirby said, is that it hurts. That means a tattoo can hurt twice: when you get it, and when you get rid of it. Of course, for teenagers with angry parents, a fresh tattoo could be painful in other ways.

American Travels

Americans are a traveling people, whether it's an actual road trip, a flight to Europe, or an armchair travel experience through scores of cable television options.

Research gathered by the U.S. Travel Association (USTA) shows that, despite recent economic turbulence, Americans still find ways to tour the country and the world, often on their own terms. For leisure travel, the automobile is the runaway winner for getaways, accounting for more than three-fourths of all such trips in a year. Air travel is second.

Families comprise almost one-third of all adult leisure travelers in the nation. Rather than just one big annual vacation, family travelers in the 21st century opt for shorter, more frequent travel: They average 4.5 trips a year.

Where they choose to go is not much different than it was for past generations.

Top 10 U.S. Travel Activities for Americans

1. Visiting friends and relatives
2. Sightseeing
3. Beaches/waterfronts
4. Zoos/aquariums/science museums
5. National parks
6. State parks
7. Cruises
8. Theme parks
9. Cities
10. Mountain areas

Source: U.S. Travel Association

Despite the allure of foreign travel, 98% of long-distance trips—any trip over 50 miles—by Americans are to places within the U.S., according to the National Household Travel Survey. And that "long-distance" label can be a bit deceiving, since nearly two-thirds of long-distance trips are to destinations in the traveler's home state. We may be willing to travel over the river and through the woods to grandmother's house, but she usually lives just down the road, or at least in the same state.

The holiday song may be appealing, but in the real world not many Americans are traveling by one-horse, open sleigh anymore. Nine of every 10 long-distance trips are taken in personal vehicles. Another 7% happen by air, 2% by bus, and 1% by train. But Americans have their limits when it comes to how far they will ride in the family car. It's a big country, and for anything beyond 1,000 miles each way, three-fourths of Americans put the keys away and book a flight.

Business Travel

Not all travel is just for fun. Business purposes accounted for almost 50% of air travel in the past year by adults. Work-related travel generates nearly $250 billion in spending and 2.3 million jobs in the U.S.

Generational Travel

Why and how often Americans travel depends in part on their age. Not surprisingly, people 65 and older account for more than one in five leisure travelers in the country. But this "mature traveler" group, as the U.S. Travel Association calls them, also comprises 14% of business travelers. Maybe 65 is the new 45 when it comes to being a business road warrior.

Travelers of Gen X (born 1965 to 1980) and Gen Y (after 1980), who already represent nearly half of Americans on the road for leisure or business purposes, clearly are ready to take over the traveling torch from Baby Boomers. With their higher levels of technology use, it's clear that travel providers from airlines to hotel chains will have to be ready to meet the next generation of travelers on their digital terms.

In line with long-term demographic trends in the United States, travel is on the rise among Americans of Hispanic origin. According to *Profile of Hispanic/Latino Leisure Travelers,* there are more than 16 million Hispanic adult leisure travelers in the country. They make more than 50 million trips a year valued at nearly $60 billion in economic impact.

How Americans Plan Their Travel

To decide where to travel, and plan how to get there, Americans increasingly are turning to the Internet, which is already the top information source for leisure travel. About one-quarter of people still get information from their friends and relatives, and 15% of leisure travelers still rely on an old-fashioned travel reference: the guide book. But 90 million American adults use the Internet to plan their trips.

Their use of technology for travel purposes isn't limited to tools for deciding where to go and for booking the trip. Smart phones, including iPhones, BlackBerrys, Androids, and other varieties, are being used more often by people during travel, according to the 2010 *Portrait of American Travelers.*

One in five U.S. travelers has downloaded a travel-related application to their smart phone. Nearly half of them use GPS maps in their smart phones to find where they are or where they are going, and roughly the same number check flight schedules and delays from the palm of their hands. An increasing number, now 29% but likely to grow, do their travel booking comparison shopping via smart phone, bypassing the computer altogether. And some smart phone travelers have travel coupons on their phones (11%) or use the smart phone to download and play an audio walking tour (6%).

After they get back home, Americans aren't done using the Internet for travel. Nearly 90% of people with incomes over $50,000 have used Facebook for such things as posting or viewing travel photos and information or writing reviews for other travelers.

A 2010 Ypartnership/Harrison Group study of American travelers with household incomes over $50,000 found that all trips aren't planned so carefully or use such high-tech means. Nearly a third in this travel market admit taking a last-minute trip during the past year, hitting the road an average of only six days after getting the travel bug.

Americans show every sign that they plan to keep traveling. One of seven people in the study said they'd like to buy a vacation home, and about half that many are interested in timeshare travel.

Traveling Companions

Only one in 10 leisure travelers goes it alone, according to the USTA. Alone when it comes to other people, that is. Some solo travelers are among the 18% of U.S. adults who take a pet with them when they travel for fun. Arf!

Top Travel Destinations of Americans

For people who do most of their traveling from a favorite chair, via a book or TV show, some are fascinated by the places famous people want to travel. Hey, if you aren't going yourself, and you can pick any place to travel in your mind, why travel as yourself when you can pretend to be a movie star, professional athlete, or CEO? According to National Geographic's *My Favorite Place on Earth,* here are the places they prefer to travel:

Travel Favorites of the Rich and Famous

NBA legend Kareem Abdul-Jabbar	Trinidad
Jeopardy's Alex Trebek	Oxford and Cambridge
Author Tony Hillerman	Shiprock, New Mexico
Actor Ted Danson	Martha's Vineyard
News icon Tom Brokaw	Tibet
Cartoonist Matt Groening	Hawaii

Those sound like fine places to visit, but according to research by *Forbes Traveler,* Times Square is the No. 1 choice by Americans among all domestic travel destinations, with more than 37 million visitors in 2009 alone. That's quite a turnaround from past generations when the famed street scene was less glitz and more grunge.

The hype of the Las Vegas Strip, with 29 million visitors, and the history of the National Mall and Parks in Washington (25 million) are second and third. The rest of the top 10 destinations include:

4. Faneuil Hall Marketplace, Boston, 19 million
5. Disney's Magic Kingdom, Orlando, 17 million
6. Golden Gate National Recreation Area, San Francisco 17 million
7. Disneyland resort, Anaheim, 15 million
8. Fisherman's Wharf, San Francisco, 10 million
9. Hollywood Walk of Fame, Los Angeles, 10 million
10. Great Smoky Mountains Park, North Carolina and Tennessee, 9.5 million

Source: Forbes Traveler

With that cluster of California destinations near the top of the list, it's no surprise that the state is at the top of U.S. states visited by American tourists, according to the Travel Industry Association of America. Florida, with its theme parks and beaches, runs second, followed by Texas, New York, Pennsylvania, Illinois, Ohio, North Carolina, Georgia, and Virginia.

For those 2% of American travelers who manage to afford an international trip, U.S. Department of Transportation studies show that, in a country with so many citizens of European descent, there's still no place like home. Europe accounts for more than 40% of international trips by Americans, nearly all of it to ancestral locations in Western Europe. Asian destinations are a distant second, at nearly 20% of foreign travel, followed closely by Caribbean destinations. Central and South America, Africa, and the Middle East each account for single-digit percentages of annual travel by Americans. But with more than 25 million international travelers overall, those small groups still add up to lots of Americans seeing the world.

Outnumbered by Pets

Even when the U.S. population rises above 310 million, Americans will be outnumbered by the pets they own. Of course, most cat and dog owners will tell you that their furry friends think they are the owners, rather than the people.

According to the 2010 National Pet Owners Survey by the American Pet Products Association, the total number of pets owned in the United States included:

Animal	**U.S. Pets in Millions**
1. Freshwater fish	171.7
2. Cats	93.6
3. Dogs	77.5
4. Birds	15.0
5. Reptiles	13.6
6. Equine	13.3
7. Saltwater fish	11.2
8. Other small animals	15.9 (including 6.1 million rabbits)

The APPA estimates that Americans spent more than $47 billion on their pets in 2010, which was nearly three times the expenditures in 1994. The total tab for Tabby, Fido, and friends included:

• Food	$18 billion
• Supplies and medicine	$11 billion
• Vet care	$12 billion
• Grooming and boarding	$3 billion
• Live animal purchases	$2 billion

The average household spent more than $360 on veterinary bills in 2006—twice that much in dog and cat households—according to the American Veterinary Medical Association. That's partly because, according to the AVMA, nearly half of pet owners considered their pets to be family members! Dog owners spend $40 million, and cat owners $19 million, on toys for their pets. Cats reportedly are not amused at their toy deficit.

All Dressed Up

According to a 2010 AP-Petside.com poll, more than 45% of Americans keep photos of a pet in their wallet or cell phone. Even if the cat or dog doesn't believe in Santa Claus, 43% of American pet owners say they plan to buy their pet a holiday gift this year. Nearly a quarter of dog owners, and 12% of cat owners, have bought their pet an outfit. And 25% of people say their pet is a better listener than their spouse.

Where They Come From

According to the National Pet Owners Survey, 62% of households have at least one pet. Most people in those 71 million homes get pets from friends or family members. But the American Society for the Prevention of Cruelty to Animals found that up to 20% of dogs are bought from breeders, and 10% to 20% of cats and dogs are adopted from animal shelters and rescue agencies.

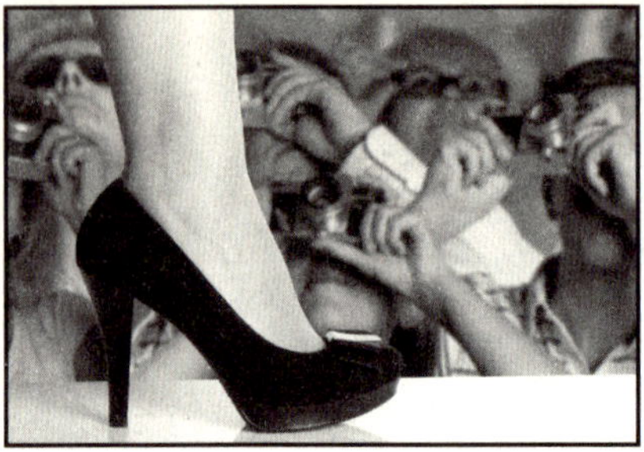

What Americans Wear

Many people have heard the familiar phrase "clothes make the man," but few can quote the rest of that Mark Twain zinger: "Clothes make the man. Naked people have little or no influence in society." Whether Twain was commenting on the relationship between apparel and social status, or just making fun of people who worry about such things, Americans still pay a great deal of attention to how they dress.

According to the American Apparel and Footwear Association, people donned more than 19 billion garments in 2008. That included 2.2 billion pairs of shoes, an average of seven pairs for every man, woman, and child in the country.

Business Casual

Millions of jobs that used to require suit jackets, ties, and dresses now allow more casual attire at work. Ipsos, a market research company, found that 37% of Americans still work in traditional business attire, but more people (41%) now wear casual clothes. Half of those who participated in the survey thought casual attire makes workers more productive. About one in five said that a casually dressed worker is just a "slacker."

Heels and Hemlines

Despite widespread acceptance of comfortable footwear for women, an American Podiatric Association survey found that 39% of women wear high heels every day. They keep putting on those heels despite the fact that three-quarters of them experience back pain and foot ailments.

Nearly a century ago, economist George Taylor described the "hemline index," which suggested that dress lengths rose and fell with the economy. According to Bloomberg News, some economists and fashion experts have matched the so-called index to periods of economic expansion and contraction, such as the Great Depression and the economic boom of the 1960s. During the recent U.S. recession and 57% decline in the S&P stock index, historian Daniel James Cole claimed to see young New Yorkers wearing long dresses for the first time in years.

School Uniforms

The National Center for Education Statistics found that 18% of U.S. public schools require students to wear uniforms. Even if uniforms aren't required, most students today (55%) are held to a strict dress code of some kind. To meet those needs, today's average American family spends over $600 per child on clothing, shoes, and school supplies and equipment.

(Bare) Vacation Wear

What Americans wear on their vacations can vary widely, depending on whether it's ski season or a trip to the beach. But a 2010 online survey by the travel website TripAdvisor found that a surprising number of people (48%) are open to wearing nothing at all on vacation—provided the locale is a clothing-optional site.

Our Eating Habits

For early American settlers, the search for food was often a central part of daily life, and success wasn't guaranteed. Today, it's hard to walk 10 feet without practically falling over a food opportunity. The big challenge of the 21st century is making the healthiest use of those chances, rather than surviving.

A CBS News poll in 2010 showed that three-fourths of Americans still eat together regularly as a family. That aligns with a finding by the *Journal of American Medicine:* more than 40% of people claim they eat together every day.

What has changed in recent years, however, is the number of distractions a family may experience. According to the poll, a third of people keep the TV on during dinner. One in 20 uses a cell phone during dinner to text or e-mail someone.

Breakfast Habits

According to the USDA, four of every five Americans eat breakfast. The age groups most likely to eat breakfast are the very young (ages two to five), at 95%, and people 70 and older, at 92%. One-fourth of Americans eat breakfast away from home on any given day, and they aren't as likely to eat healthy food when they are on the run. Only 9% of Americans munch on ready-to-eat cereals when they eat away from home. Instead, they are more likely to eat fried potatoes, sweet rolls, bacon, sausage, and breakfast sandwiches.

Snacking

After breakfast, a significant number of Americans get through the rest of the school or work day in part by snacking. The USDA says that 83% of teens eat at least one snack a day, and those snacks deliver nearly one-fourth of their daily caloric intake. That's a big change since the 1970s, when the snacking percentage among teens was 61%.

That's not the only eating habit that has changed in recent decades. According to *Eating Patterns in America*, published by NPD Group:

- Americans now eat more take-out meals in their cars than they do at work—the reverse of the take-out ratio in 1984.
- Salads are now part of only 16% of dinners at home, compared to 22% in 1984.
- Fewer of us eat donuts for breakfast—10% now compared to 17% in 1989.

The NPD study found that although people eat many of the same foods they ate 30 years ago, somebody else is often doing the cooking. For example, sandwiches are still common, but now the sandwich is less likely to be made by a family member and more likely to come from a restaurant or other ready-to-eat source. Nearly 60% of main courses for dinner are still cooked from scratch, but that's down from 72% a generation ago, and the decline is expected to continue.

The microwave now plays a role in preparing twice as many meals as in the 1980s, when that time-saving device was relatively new to the American kitchen. But quick zapping is not the only labor-saving cooking option that has grown in use. Slow-cookers are used 67% more often now than in the '80s.

According to NPD Group, there are more than 578,000 restaurants in the country. Of those, more than half are fast-food restaurants, according to the *American Journal of Public Health.* When Americans eat out, a 2007 CBS News survey revealed, the hamburger is still king, often accompanied by fries.

Top 5 Restaurant Food Choices

1. Hamburgers
2. French fries
3. Pizza
4. Mexican food
5. Chicken sandwiches

If you prefer to cook, you'll have little trouble finding groceries. The Food Marketing Institute estimates the country has more than 35,000 supermarkets, defined as a grocery store with at least $2 million in annual sales. And despite those of us who seem to make a grocery trip just about every day because we forgot something, the FMI says the average consumer makes two grocery trips a week.

The recent American Time Use Survey found that Americans 15 and older spend more than an hour a day eating food and drinking beverages as a primary activity—at a sit-down meal or other food-focused time. But that's not the whole story. People also spend at least 15 minutes a day eating and another 40 minutes drinking something as a secondary activity, while doing something like working or watching TV.

Eating in Space

America's manned space program has come a long way since the days when early astronauts ate unappetizing food that had been cubed or freeze-dried, or had to be squeezed from a tube. According to NASA.com, today's astronauts eat three meals a day that have been carefully planned by nutritionists and customized for each astronaut's gender and body weight.

The astronauts' options include "fruits, nuts, peanut butter, chicken, beef, seafood, candy, brownies" as well as "coffee, tea, orange juice, fruit punches, and lemonade." Don't look for salt and pepper shakers in space. Those and other seasonings and condiments are only available in liquid form in order to avoid the mess of powdered or granulated items floating around in zero gravity.

Selected Favorite Foods of U.S. Presidents

George Washington	hazelnuts, cherries, game
Thomas Jefferson	sweet potatoes, ham, soufflés, wine
Abraham Lincoln	apples, eggs, coffee
Teddy Roosevelt	boiled eggs, grits, steak
Franklin D. Roosevelt	creamed chipped beef, soups
Harry Truman	roast, fried chicken
John F. Kennedy	poached eggs, soups, lamb chops
Jimmy Carter	pork chops, grits, peanuts
Ronald Reagan	soups, jelly beans
Bill Clinton	tacos, ribs, cheeseburgers
George W. Bush	Tex-Mex foods, biscuits
Barack Obama	trail mix, chocolate, tea

Source: The Food Timeline

Restaurant Etiquette

That $5 you left on the counter may not seem like much, but it's part of more than $20 billion in tip income each year for servers and other restaurant workers.

Cornell University researchers have found that the average tip in America is nearly 18%, but actual tips vary widely for a number of reasons. Although tipping may be influenced by service, food quality, social expectations, and even the day of the week, studies have found that American restaurant servers get bigger tips if they:

- introduce themselves
- smile
- tell jokes
- use the customer's name
- write "thank you" notes or draw pictures on the bill
- sit during order-taking to be on the same level as the customer
- repeat what customers say when ordering

Contrary to what many people believe, researchers have found that there's not much difference in tipping based on the gender of the server and the customer. But other factors, such as how much alcohol diners consume, still matter.

Gallup poll results shed light on who is tipping—or not tipping—among Americans:

41% Women who say tips should be 20% or more
30% Men who agree with 20%-or-more tips
49% High-income diners favoring 20% tips
35% Middle-income diners who believe in 20% tips
25% Lower-income 20% tippers
46% People who have left no tip due to poor service

Married people often disagree—no surprise there—about who tips better. Half of married men say they tip more; 38% of married women say they tip more than their husbands.

Smoking in Bars and Restaurants

A 2010 Gallup survey found that the tide continues to run against smoking in restaurants. Nearly 60% of Americans now say that governments should ban the practice. That opposition has nearly tripled since Gallup first asked the question in 1987. But a majority of people still think smoking is all right in bars: Nearly one-fourth are okay with no restrictions at all, while 43% want designated smoking areas in bars.

Don't Answer That

A Harris Interactive poll found that more than half of Americans have been bothered by somebody using a cell phone in a restaurant. But only 28% of people admitted that they talk on the phone while dining out. It sounds like some of the offenders were too embarrassed to own up to their restaurant rudeness.

How We Entertain Ourselves

Somewhere, in a room that may or may not have windows, somebody has the job of measuring what Americans do in their spare time—and how often they do it. Before you look at what they came up with, tip your hat to the leisure-activity counting office and wish them all a chance to go to the park and fly a kite sometime soon.

The Census Bureau includes among its myriad publications a table of *Adult Participation in Selected Leisure Activities by Frequency.* The data, collected by Mediamark Research & Intelligence, fortunately doesn't cover *everything* Americans do for fun, but it does paint a picture of a nation that has no trouble staying busy.

The statistics cover nearly 50 different activities during 2008. Since people are creatures of habit, there's a good chance these activities are still going on in your town. They range from attending horse races to playing backgammon to singing karaoke. This sample doesn't include many activities covered elsewhere in this unofficial census.

Backgammon, anyone? For more than 400,000 Americans, the answer is yes—at least once a week. Those must be the hardcore fans.

Another 3.5 million adults said they played the board game at least once in the past year. Or maybe the one-tenth who play weekly are winning so often that the other 90% won't play anymore.

Some backgammon losers may have moved on to chess (7.9 million Americans per year), card games (45 million), or trivia (12 million). If the weather cooperates, others go fly a kite. Some 5.8 million adults a year pretend to let their kids fly kites, when in truth a few of the grownups are just using their children as a cover for their own fun.

When the children have entangled the kite in a tree, or the wind stops blowing, many families head to the zoo. More than 2 million adults go to a zoo every month, and more than 10 times that number say hello to the lions, tigers, and gift shops at least once a year.

More than 24 million Americans have a picnic once a year or more. Other outdoor activities people love include bird watching (14 million) and horse racing (6 million). Of course, only a small number of jockeys and trainers are actually engaged in horse racing. The other people are usually standing along a rail, holding a betting ticket and a hot dog, and mumbling something like, "I don't care if you are a 30-to-1 long-shot—run faster!"

Annual Participation	**Activity**
89 million	entertain friends or relatives at home
76 million	barbecue
52 million	bake
46 million	cook for fun
35 million	board games
32 million	crossword puzzles
29 million	video games
28 million	photography
28 million	museums
27 million	live theater
26 million	home decoration and furnishing

25 million	other music performances
24 million	rock music performances
21 million	billiards/pool
19 million	auto shows
18 million	art galleries or art shows
18 million	photo albums/scrapbooks
17 million	musical instrument
14 million	adult education courses
14 million	paint, draw
11 million	country music performances
10 million	classical music/opera performances
10 million	woodworking
9 million	bingo
8 million	concerts on radio
9 million	dance performances
7 million	book clubs
7 million	furniture refinishing
5 million	comic books

Source: Adult Participation in Selected Leisure Activities by Frequency

Once the sun goes down and the kids are in bed, holding their $29 stuffed tiger from the zoo and wondering what happened to the kite, adults often find something else to occupy their leisure time. At least once a week, 25 million adults go out to eat and 8 million go to a bar. Nearly 3 million have the energy to go dancing two or three times a month. A few probably manage to do all three things in one night.

Other studies confirm that Americans find plenty to entertain themselves even during times of economic distress. The National Endowment for the Arts (NEA) estimates that one in three adults goes to an art museum or a live arts performance at least once a year. Roughly one-quarter of people surveyed choose art museums or galleries. Ballet and opera companies attract 7 million and 5 million people, respectively, each year.

In the digital age, some people who aren't able to get out to a play or symphony use their computers to enjoy art, according to the NEA. Nearly one in five adults who visit the Internet have used it to view paintings, sculptures, or photography. And nearly one-third of Internet users in America report listening to music or watching theater or dance performances online.

Several types of popular cable television shows seem to confirm the most common things Americans do to entertain themselves. With the number of cooking icons on TV, from to Emeril to Paula Dean, is it any surprise that surveys show that more than 50 million Americans say that baking is a leisure activity, not a necessity?

Nearly that many see cooking in general as entertainment, or at least as relaxation. And when it's not snowing or raining, more than 75 million can't wait to fire up the grill. If you ask any two of those barbecuing millions whether coal or gas grilling is better, or what type of smoker is best, you should step back to avoid getting barbecue sauce on your shirt.

Depending on which person you ask, home improvement is either a leisure activity or a list of things your significant other makes to fill your weekend. Either way, 26 million Americans engage in home decorating and furnishing for fun, and another 10 million participate in woodworking. Once again, TV shows reflect the fascination: *This Old House, Trading Spaces, Flip This House,* and *New Yankee Workshop* are just a few places people go to watch other people show them how to give their home a makeover or stay out of trouble in the woodshop.

Spectator Sports in America

Americans have always been crazy about sports, and 21st century fans are taking their fanaticism to new levels and activities. The Census Bureau's collected attendance figures from professional and college sports organizations show significant growth in popularity among most sports categories over the past 20 years.

Despite the high price of tickets to Major League Baseball games, and disaffection among fans for unethical behavior by some players during the steroid era, America's pastime continues to fill seats at most stadiums. In 2010, Major League Baseball drew more than 73 million fans, an average of more than 30,000 per game. That's a lot of peanuts and Cracker Jacks—and baseball caps and other souvenirs—but observers note that attendance is down from a record high in 2007 of nearly 80 million fans.

Professional basketball and hockey franchises have struggled more in recent years to fill seats, according to ESPN and other sources. But that's not to say these aren't still lucrative businesses capable of paying star athletes millions of dollars a year. The average National Basketball Association game attracts more than 17,000 fans, and the average NBA franchise is worth more than $360 million, according to *Forbes*. Dramatic growth for professional basketball in international markets, including China and Europe, is expected to keep the cash register ringing. Hockey pulls in as many fans as the NBA, over the same number of regular season games.

But the National Football League has become king of the hill among American spectator sports in recent years. With average per-game attendance of more than 67,000 fans, and millions more watching on television every week, the NFL is making a serious run at long-term dominance for fan attention. Super Bowl Sunday has become a red-letter date on the entertainment calendar for many Americans. More than 100 million people tune in to part or all of the telecast of the big game, according to Nielsen.

Fantasy Sports

Fueled in large part by the Internet, an increasing number of Americans entertain themselves through fantasy sports leagues instead of only attending or watching games to cheer for one team. Fantasy sports games, in which participants compete to select the best-performing individual players in a sport, involve more than 27 million Americans, according to Reuters. And fantasy leagues have become a big business, accounting for the spending of nearly $1 billion on related products and contest fees. The gender gap among fantasy players has narrowed in recent years, but men are still three of every four participants, and they spend 90% of the money involved.

The fact that Americans love fantasy sports doesn't mean participants aren't supporting their teams in person. Only 12% of all Americans attend at least one Major League Baseball game a season, but nearly 80% of fantasy sports players go to ballgames. The numbers are similar for football and basketball.

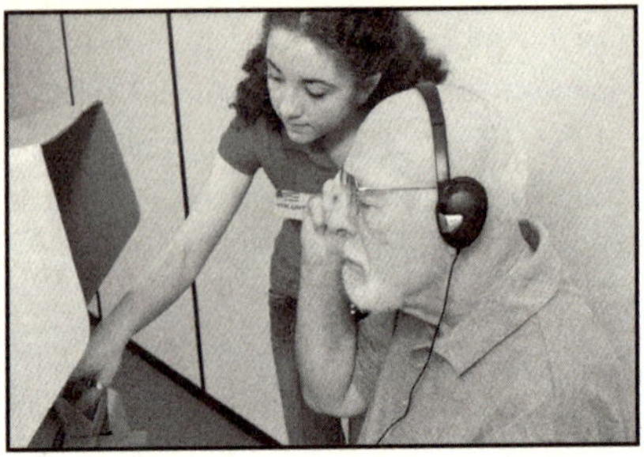

Volunteer Nation

Americans are often accused of being self-centered, but national volunteerism statistics tell a different story. In fact, from retired people to children, in big cities to small towns, Americans give generously of their time. Moreover, they continued to do so even in the face of the recent economic downturn.

In 2009, 63.4 million Americans volunteered in their communities, according to the Corporation for National and Community Service. Their combined community service surpassed 8 billion hours in one year and was valued at nearly $170 billion.

Religious organizations attracted the biggest share of all U.S. volunteer work (35.6%). Schools and other educational causes were next with more than 26%. Other causes that received help included social services, health, civic, sports, arts, and others.

The Faces of Volunteers

Women (30%) are more likely to volunteer than men (23%). Nearly one-third of adults from ages 35 to 54 volunteer, a higher rate than for younger and older Americans. However, participation is growing among all age groups. Despite their household responsibilities, people with young children volunteer at high rates, often for groups that their children belong to.

The more people learn, and the more they earn, the more likely they are to volunteer—in part due to more time and opportunity. Nearly 43% of college graduates volunteer, compared with just under 19% of high school graduates and only 8.6% of Americans with less education.

Employed people (30%) pitch in more frequently than those not in the work force (23%). It's no surprise that part-time workers are more likely to participate than their full-time coworkers.

Some occupations have especially high levels of volunteer participation, particularly when there's a chance to do community work that uses the volunteer's professional skills. People may tell a lot of jokes about lawyers, but the punch line here is that 36% of them give free legal help to organizations or individuals in need—and legal professionals have one of the highest overall volunteer rates (47%) of any field. That's true partly because the American Bar Association encourages its members to provide at least 50 hours of pro bono legal work each year.

Teachers and librarians find it a natural fit to use their skills in volunteering: More than a third of them tutor or teach people for free. More than 36% of farmers, fishers, foresters, miners, and construction workers contribute free labor or transportation to their favorite volunteer cause.

Where the Volunteers Are

Some cities and states have higher rates of participation in volunteer work than others. The Corporation for National and Community Service found that home ownership, education level, poverty rate, and other factors were related to volunteerism.

Highest Rate of Volunteer Participation, States

1. Utah
2. Iowa
3. Minnesota
4. Nebraska
5. Alaska

Even in states at the bottom of the ranking, residents were no slouches at volunteering. New York, Nevada, New Jersey, Louisiana, Florida, and Mississippi all had at or near 20% participation.

Highest Rate of Volunteer Participation, Big Cities

1. Minneapolis–St. Paul
2. Portland, OR
3. Salt Lake City
4. Seattle
5. Oklahoma City

Highest Rate of Volunteer Participation, Midsize Cities

1. Provo, UT
2. Iowa City, IA
3. Ogden, UT
4. Fort Collins, CO
5. Madison, WI

Going the Distance to Volunteer

One striking fact about American volunteers is how far some of them are willing to travel to help other people. In 2007, 3.7 million people traveled at least 120 miles to do volunteer work in the United States. Not surprisingly, young adults ages 16 to 24, who are less likely to be married or have children, account for a higher proportion of traveling volunteers than other age groups.

To Get Volunteers, Just Ask—Or Don't

A 2009 study revealed that 44% of people get involved as volunteers for their chosen cause after someone asked them to help. But, surprisingly, nearly 41% just showed up to volunteer on their own, without being asked.

Once they show up, the typical volunteer spends approximately one hour per week helping out, according to the corporation's findings. For Americans over 65, who have more time to give, the median annual volunteer time is highest, at 90 hours a year.

People spend more time raising money (11%) for their cause than any other activity. That's followed by jobs related to food, including collecting, preparing, or serving meals.

Top U.S. Volunteer Activities by Gender

Activity	Men	Women
General labor	12.4%	5.8%
Coach or referee	9.4%	2.6%
Fundraising	9.4%	9.4%
Food service	11.8%	8.2%
Tutor or teacher	11.0%	7.3%

Volunteering May Cut into TV Watching Time

One recent survey found that Americans who volunteer spend nearly an hour less each day watching television. It may not sound like much, but that's an extra 300-plus hours of volunteer time a year.

The Longer the Commute, the Less Time There Is to Volunteer

States with short average commuting times—such as North Dakota (16.0 minutes), South Dakota (16.4 minutes), Montana (17.9 minutes), and Nebraska (18.0 minutes)—consistently have participation rates over 35%. By comparison, the rates dip below 30% in states like New Jersey and in cities like Chicago, where the average commute is more than 30 minutes.

Embracing the Arts

Americans love art. According to the most recent Survey of Public Participation in the Arts by the National Endowment for the Arts (2008), a significant number of Americans paint, draw, sculpt, sing, dance, or play a musical instrument.

Number of U.S. Adults Performing or Creating Art

Play an instrument	28.4 million
Jazz	3.1 million
Classical music	6.9 million
Opera	0.8 million
Choir/chorale	11.6 million
Musical plays	2 million
Non-musical plays	1.7 million
Dance	4.8 million
Paint/draw/sculpt	20.1 million
Pottery/jewelry	13.4 million
Weaving/sewing	29.5 million

Another 45 million Americans own original artworks created by others, and roughly 13 million people buy a piece of art each year. According to the NEA, approximately 2.1% of adults take a visual arts class, 1.7% take a music lesson, and 1.4% take a creative writing class.

The 2009 Public Attitudes Towards Music study, conducted by Gallup for the National Association of Music Merchants, found that Americans believe that the benefits for children and teenagers of playing an instrument include:

97% developing creativity
96% developing teamwork skills from playing in a school band
94% developing a child's intellect
94% relieving stress and providing relaxation
93% making friends
88% improving grades and encouraging kids to stay in school

A number of prominent American public figures have devoted time in their personal lives to playing a musical instrument. Former President Bill Clinton (saxophone), economist and former Federal Reserve Chairman Alan Greenspan (clarinet), former U.S. Secretary of State Condoleeza Rice (piano), and legendary physicist Albert Einstein (piano, violin) have the makings of a pretty good amateur band among them.

According to a Gallup survey for the International Music Products Association, more than half of U.S. households have at least one person who plays an instrument. And the prospects are good that Americans will continue to make music for decades to come. Of those who play, one-third are between the ages of five and 17, and another one-quarter are 18 to 34.

Sports Participation and Outdoor Activities

America is a nation of weekend warriors—and sometimes weeknight warriors, too. Despite being heavily scheduled on weekdays for work or classes, a significant number of people find time and energy to run, kick, swim, coach, climb, and generally compete with others and with themselves.

Hundreds of thousands of families head for playgrounds and gyms each week to watch their young children learn the basics of soccer, football, basketball, and baseball. By the time they are in high school, many young Americans are ready to compete at a higher level. According to the National Federation of State High School Associations, more than 7 million boys and girls participate in at least one high school athletic program every year.

That number has steadily increased with few exceptions over the past 30 years, but the biggest participation gains have been among females: from 1.75 million girls playing high school sports in 1980 to more than 3 million today.

Participation in Selected U.S. High School Sports

Sport	Male	Female
Football	1.1 million	—
Basketball	556,000	457,000
Track and field	544,000	444,000
Baseball	477,000	—
Softball	—	373,000
Golf	160,000	66,000
Tennis	157,000	177,000
Swimming/diving	107,000	144,000

Source: National Federation of State High School Associations

Friday night high school football games are the biggest thing going in hundreds of communities across the nation. But the next morning, many adults who cheered for the local team, win or lose, turn to a different competition: the battle to control their lawns and gardens. According to the National Gardening Association (NGA), 70% of U.S. households spend some time—and more than $36 billion a year—on lawn and garden efforts. Nearly a quarter of them attempt to raise their own vegetables. Other findings by the 2008 NGA study include:

Lawn/Garden Activity	Households Engaged
Lawn care	46%
Flowers	32%
Houseplants	31%
Landscaping	28%
Shrubs	22%
Herbs	12%
Fruit trees	10%
Berries	6%

Source: The National Gardening Association

For other Americans, cutting the grass will have to wait if the weather is good on the weekend. It's time to tee off and play a round of golf at one of the nation's nearly 16,000 courses. The National Sporting Goods Association (NSGA) estimates that more than 22 million Americans play golf. Three times as many men as women play.

The most common physical activities for Americans, however, are walking for exercise (56 million women and 33 million men) and exercising with equipment at home or in a gym (a combined 86 million).

Other amateur sporting activities that engage at least 20 million Americans on a regular basis include basketball, bike riding, billiards, bowling, camping, fishing, running, swimming, boating, and target shooting.

More than 7 million Americans like nothing better than to wear camouflage outfits, sneak around an indoor or outdoor facility, and shoot each other with paintball guns. The NSGA found that a surprising 50,000 of those paintball warriors are age 65 or older. So much for bingo.

Slightly more than 12 million people participate in amateur dart throwing. Since many dartboards are located in a local bar, it's a good guess that those participants may be holding a dart in one hand and a beverage in the other.

Running Events

Running or jogging attracts more than 30 million Americans a year, almost evenly divided between male and female runners. They get started young, too. More than 2 million runners are age seven to 11, and another 5 million are age 12 to 17. Organized running events are popular at distances ranging from one-mile fun runs to 5K and 10K events to full-fledged marathons.

Millions of people get the idea every year to train for and attempt to complete a marathon (26.2 miles). After months of training, the majority of first-time entrants are able to finish. But many of them check the marathon off their list of life goals and go back to shorter races—or dart throwing, for that matter. The continual infusion of first-time marathoners, along with a core of regular participants, has helped several large-scale marathons thrive for decades. They include the Marine Corps Marathon, which winds past the monuments and national institutions of Washington, D.C.; the New York City Marathon, through the boroughs of the city that never sleeps; the Chicago and Orlando marathons; and the pinnacle of distance racing for American runners, the Boston Marathon.

The Boston Marathon draws more than 26,000 runners, many of whom had to meet difficult qualifying times in other marathons in order to run at Boston. Ironically, although a Boston Marathon runner's number is the most sought after for American amateur runners, no American has won the event since 1985 (Lisa Rainsberger). The Boston race and numerous other major marathons worldwide are often dominated by Kenyan elite runners.

Many Americans combine their enjoyment of organized running events with their passion for supporting good causes. Nearly every American town with more than a few hundred people hosts at least one 5K or other road race each year that raises money or awareness for a local charity or national cause.

Volunteers and runners have participated for more than 25 years in the Susan G. Komen Race for the Cure, the world's largest series of 5K runs and fitness walks. Komen races and other programs have raised hundreds of millions of dollars for breast cancer research. More than 1 million Americans participate in a Komen race every year.

Adventure Racing and Triathlons

For some people, running 26 miles and a few more feet through a big city, with bands playing and friends and family cheering them on, just isn't enough of a challenge. According to the Sporting Goods

Manufacturers Association, more than 780,000 people participated in adventure races in the United States in 2009.

Adventure racing usually combines two or more endurance activities. Orienteering or navigation is always included, and it's combined with one or more challenging outdoor activities such as cross-country running, mountain biking, paddling, or climbing. Adventure races can last from two hours to more than a week, depending on the event and the lunacy of the racers.

Other endurance sports participants are less excited about the orienteering part of adventure racing. Or maybe they just have a bad sense of direction. Whatever the reason, these people direct their energy toward the triathlon, a sequence of swimming, cycling, and running over various distances.

The SGMA has estimated that nearly 700,000 people participate in triathlons around the United States every year. USA Triathlon sanctions more than 2,000 triathlon events in the country and has more than 100,000 members. The inclusion of the triathlon as an Olympic event for the first time in 2000 sparked new interest in the sport and contributed to a fivefold increase in USAT membership.

The first decade of the 21st century saw rapid growth in participation in other sports and fitness activities, too. The SGMA, which tracks participation rates in various sports, says that Pilates training has by far seen the greatest increase, surging by nearly 500% from 2000 to 2007. More than 9 million Americans now include Pilates training in their fitness routines.

Another low-impact form of exercise, elliptical motion training, increased by more than 220% in the same period. So many fitness centers have added elliptical training devices in recent years that it's hard to find a gym without one. Nearly 24 million Americans use them, including many people whose knees or feet can't handle the pounding that is a byproduct of running.

Other sports and fitness activities with high growth in participation since 2000 include:

Activity	Participants	Increase
Yoga/Tai Chi	14 million	125%
Lacrosse	1 million	104%
Paintball	5 million	52%
Stretching	36 million	47%
Treadmill	50 million	34%
Spinning	6 million	34%
Running	41 million	31%
Tennis	17 million	31%

Source: SGMA

Camping and Hiking

Plenty of people go into the woods of America every weekend without any intention of racing up a hill or careening through the trails during a mountain bike event. They just want to go camping. No freeway traffic, office phones, or spreadsheets. The NSGA estimates that more than 47 million participate in camping of some kind every year. The family-oriented nature of this weekend activity is clear: More than 9 million of the participants are children. While enjoying the great outdoors, many of these same people participate in hiking, which attracts nearly 30 million people.

For people who want a little more action while in the wilderness, other popular activities on the weekend include hunting (25 million) and fishing (35 million).

How Americans Get Around

The 1989 film depiction of 2015 America in *Back to the Future II* included two memorable means of futuristic transportation: flying skateboards and a flying version of the stylish DeLorean time machine. With only a short time before the real 2015 arrives, there's no real-world sign yet of Marty McFly's fictional means of getting around, but Americans today manage to cover a lot of miles anyway.

The National Household Travel Survey, released after the 2000 U.S. Census, estimated that Americans make more than a billion trips of all kinds every day, and studies since then have shown that people are not cutting back. That's an average of more than three trips for every person in the nation, totaling 11 billion miles a day!

The vast majority of those trips are in cars, trucks, and other personal vehicles, although those are not the only options.

Fast Facts on American Transportation

Americans make:

- 411 billion daily trips a year, totaling 4 trillion miles

- 45% of their trips are for errands, including shopping
- 14% of their trips are for commuting to and from work

Personal Vehicles in the U.S.

Type	Number
Cars/station wagons	116 million
Vans and SUVs	43 million
Light trucks	39 million

Source: National Household Travel Survey

Sometime in the past decade, there were—for the first time—more personal vehicles per household (1.9) in the nation than there were drivers per household (1.8), according to the Bureau of Transportation Statistics. Only 8% of households in the U.S. don't have a vehicle at all. Many of the people living in those homes are among the 17% of Americans who use public transportation.

Planes, Trains, Buses, Boats, and More

When they aren't driving or riding in a personal vehicle, Americans often are passengers in larger modes of transport. The millions of conveyances that carry people and goods in the country include:

Vehicle	Number
General aviation planes	229,000
Motorcycles	7.8 million
Motor buses	63,000
Light rail cars	1,900
Heavy rail cars	11,000
Trolley buses	600
Commuter rail cars, locomotives	6,500
Rail freight cars	1.4 million
Rail locomotive	24,000

Amtrak passenger cars	1,150
Amtrak locomotives	275
Non-self-propelled boats	31,000
Self-propelled boats	9,000
Large ocean vessels	270
Recreational boats	12.5 million

Source: U.S. Department of Transportation

In an era of volatile prices for gasoline, some Americans look for cheaper ways of traveling, especially for short trips around town that don't require high speeds or large cargo space. Several types of light electric vehicles, or LEVs, have gained some ground among consumers, according to the Internet site Electric-Bikes.com. Among them:

Light Electric Vehicle	Speed (mph)
Electric scooters	10–15
Electric bicycles	12–20
Electric tricycles (adult three-wheel)	10
Electric recumbent bikes	20–35
Electric motor scooters and motorcycles	20–45
Neighborhood electric vehicles	25
One-person commuter cars	40–70
Electric pedicabs	10–20
Power-assist wheelchairs	7
Electric go-karts	5–25
Utility/Cargo Vehicles	10–40

Source: Electric-Bikes.com

Bikes and Skates

The National Bicycle Dealers Association estimates that more than 38 million Americans ages seven and older ride a bike at least six times a year. The industry sells approximately 18 million new bicycles a year, nearly all of them made in China or Taiwan. According to a survey by the Bureau of Transportation Statistics, reasons for cycling include:

Purpose for Cycling	% of trips
Recreation	26.0%
Health	23.6%
To get home	14.2%
Personal errands	13.9%
Visit friends/relatives	10.1%
Commuting (school/work)	5.0%
Just to ride a bike	2.3%
Other reasons	4.9%

National Highway Traffic Safety (NHTS) statistics show that approximately 700 Americans are killed while riding a bike every year. The number of deaths has declined slightly over the past two decades, but experts say there are many other accidents involving cyclists. A half million Americans are estimated by the NHTS to visit a hospital emergency room each year as the result of a bike accident.

As if that wasn't enough to worry fans of two-wheel, self-propelled transport, there's also the problem of having your bike stolen. The National Bike Registry estimates that 1.5 million bicycles are stolen in the country each year.

In addition to bikes and other common means of transportation, some Americans use a few less conventional means of travel, including the horse-drawn buggies in scores of traditional Amish communities. Many others would like to see better modern options for transportation. A 2010 survey by the advocacy group Transportation for America found that nearly three-fourths of Americans feel they "have no choice but to drive as much as" they do. More than 80% of those surveyed believe the United States should expand the use of rail and bus transportation.

American Reading Habits

With apologies to Mark Twain for adapting his famous retort, it appears that the death of reading in America has been greatly exaggerated. Numerous studies show that reading is alive and well, despite wild claims by some and the earnest concern of some educators about America becoming a nonreading people as the result of video games, movies, TV, and shorter attention spans.

That's not to say that the reading habits of 21st century Americans are the same as their grandparents, or that there's no cause for concern.

A 2005 Gallup survey found that just under half of adults in the nation said they were then reading a book. That's twice as many as said they were reading a book in 1957, and up from 37% in 1990. Since the survey, the unexpected success of new electronic reading devices has encouraged some researchers to believe that even more people are reading.

Gallup found that more women (53%) than men (42%) are likely to be reading a book. A generation gap is evident, which is part of the reason that reading advocates worry about the next generation of book buyers: Half of people over 30 read books, compared to only 40% of adults under 30. Those with higher education read more, as you might expect. One-third of adults with a high school education or less read books; three-fourths of those with some postgraduate education do so.

Gallup also reported that, contrary to fears that movie watching cuts into book reading, the opposite appears true. Americans who didn't go to a single movie in the previous year were only 33% likely to be reading books. Yet among people who had seen a few movies in the year, 49% were reading books. Popcorn, anyone?

How Much Time Americans Spend Reading

The American Time Use Survey, gathered by the Bureau of Labor Statistics, reveals that age, race, gender, and other factors greatly affect reading habits. Women read more than men. People 55 and older spend more than twice as much time reading as younger Americans. And it's not all that surprising that people with kids in the household just don't have the time or inclination to read as much as those with empty nests.

Group	Reading on Weekdays	Reading on Weekends/Holidays
Men	.26 hours	.28 hours
Women	.41 hours	.45 hours
Households/no children	.42 hours	.48 hours
Households/with children	.19 hours	.19 hours
High school diploma	.39 hours	.32 hours
Some college	.34 hours	.47 hours
College degree	.41 hours	.56 hours

Source: 2009 American Time Use Survey

Rise of the E-book

The advent of widely available electronic book readers seems likely to bring dramatic new changes to American reading habits. So far, the changes are small, but experts say to get ready for big ones. A Harris poll in late 2010 showed that just 8% of Americans owned an electronic reading device, but another 12% were likely to get one in the next few months.

Aggressive pricing cuts and technology advances are now seen nearly every month among manufacturers of several major e-readers, including Amazon's Kindle, the Nook reader from Barnes & Noble, and Sony's Reader line. In addition, reading software is becoming more popular on other devices, such as Apple's iPad and notebook computers.

The Harris survey found that more people are reading books because of the portable electronic readers. Among owners of the devices, a third say they read 11 to 20 books a year, and one-fourth read more than 20 books a year. Other studies confirm the trend. Marketing and Research Resources found in 2010 that 40% of Americans who own e-readers say they now read more than before they owned the device.

Key Facts About Electronic Book Readers

- At least 11 million Americans own a digital reader.
- Electronic book sales were more than twice the levels in mid-2010 than during the same time the previous year.
- More than half of e-reader owners increased their purchases of e-books in the past year.
- E-reader owners read nearly three books a month, compared to roughly two books a month read by print book devotees.

More than half of Americans who own e-readers use it for reading every day. Because two-thirds of public libraries in the country now provide online check-out of electronic books by subscribers, the American Library Association and other reading organizations expect virtual library visits to continue to rise.

A survey by the National Endowment for the Arts shows other alternative ways Americans find to consume literature and other reading material. The 2008 Survey of Public Participation in the Arts (SPPA) revealed that approximately 22 million Americans had listened to a live or recorded novel, short story, or poem during the previous year. The SPPA confirmed the trend toward online reading: 42% of all adults said they read or download Internet content including blogs, articles, or essays. A smaller group, 15%, said they read literature online.

Alternative Reading

Number	Americans' Reading Behavior
22 million	Consume live or recorded literature during a year
42%	Adults who read Internet blogs, articles, essays
15%	Adults who use the Internet to read literature

Source: Survey of Public Participation in the Arts

What Kids Are Reading, and Why

Despite some positive trends, a 2010 study by the publishing company Scholastic and the research company Harrison Group shows that books have stiff competition these days from other childhood activities. The *2010 Kids and Family Reading Report* found that children ages six to 17 spend less time each year reading for fun and more time using computers or cell phones.

Parents and their children have always seen the world through different eyes, and modern reading attitudes are no different. One in four children ages nine to 17 believes that sending and receiving text messages on a cell phone should count as "reading," but only one in 12 parents agrees. Parents and their kids at least agree on giving actual electronic book devices a chance to gain traction. More than half of children surveyed expressed interest in reading an e-book, and 83% of parents who own e-readers are willing to share them with their children.

The problem, researchers say, is that only one in 10 parents actually owns such a device. As that number grows, and the purchase of e-readers for children becomes more common, electronic reading may become more popular with the younger set.

Other Key Facts from the *2010 Kids and Family Reading Report*

- Twenty-eight percent of children nine to 17 think looking through postings or comments on social networking sites like Facebook counts as reading; only 15% of parents agree.
- A quarter of kids six to 17 say they have read a book on a digital device—most of the time on a desktop or portable computer, not on a dedicated e-reader.
- Forty-three percent of kids and parents say that, when reading books for fun, it is most important for children's imaginations to be expanded. About a third say the most important outcome is for children to gain inspiration through characters and storylines (36% of kids, 35% of parents). About one in five say it is to gain information (21% of kids, 22% of parents).
- Eighty-six percent of kids feel a sense of accomplishment when they finish reading a book.
- Only half of kids agree that reading books for fun is extremely or very important, compared to nine of 10 parents.
- Nearly three-quarters of parents wish their children would read more books for fun. The same percentage of children say they know they should read more, too.

The Business of Publishing

According to the U.S. Bureau of Labor Statistics, the average American spends only about $120 a year on reading, compared to more than $2,700 on other types of entertainment. For the newspaper industry, that trend is worrisome, to say the least.

Competition with Internet sites both for advertising dollars and published content has caused the recent business troubles of major newspapers in the U.S. The Audit Bureau of Circulations has tracked a steady fall in newspaper circulation before, during, and after the recession of 2008 and 2009. Some of the declines have been breathtaking in their speed and scale. During just one 12-month period ending in early 2010, circulation dropped by 23% at the *San Francisco Chronicle,* and major national papers including *The Washington Post* and *USA Today* saw double-digit losses.

To survive, newspapers will have to meet their readers online, of course. They are trying. The Newspaper Association of America reports that from 2005 to 2009, visits to online newspaper sites nearly doubled to more than 71 million visits. Thank goodness, because during that same period, revenues for print newspapers dropped from $22.2 billion to just over $12 billion.

Love, Sex, and Family

Hooking Up and Shacking Up in America

Dating Games

The real American dating game can be as confusing to the players as it is to those who only watch. Online matchmaking, speed dating, and even AARP dating advice are just a few bewildering signs of the times.

Millions of American singles are not in committed relationships. According to the Pew Internet & American Life Project, one in six singles is looking for a partner. Of those who are looking:

- More than one-third had not been on a date in three months.
- 13% had been on one date.
- 22% had been on two to four dates.
- One-quarter had been on five or more dates.

To improve their track record, some look for new ways to meet people. One way is "speed dating" events, where participants move from table to table with a time-limited chance to strike up a conversation with each potential partner in the room.

Click "Yes" for a Movie Date with Me

With the advent of online dating services, finding Mr. or Ms. Right has become a $1 billion business.

A *Barron's–Wall Street Journal* analysis of the Internet dating industry in 2010 found that the two biggest players are eHarmony and Match.com. Some other sites include specialty dating networks for African Americans, Jewish single people, Christian singles, and True.com, which checks the criminal history and marital status of prospective matches.

Five Top Internet Dating Sites

Site	Monthly Fee	Estimated Monthly Visitors
Match.com	$17.99–$34.99	6.9 million
eHarmony	$19.95–$59.95	3.4 million
True.com	$28.95–$59.95	3.0 million
ChristianCafe	$9.16–$34.95	950,000
JDate	$25.00–$39.99	430,000

Sources: Barron's–Wall Street Journal*; NeXt Up! Research; comScore*

The Best May Be Yet to Come, But So Is the Baggage

The American Association of Retired Persons (AARP) surveyed members in their 50s about their dating challenges.

Top Complaints About Dating by People Over 50

Men

1. Partners with "baggage": 42%
2. Those who are difficult to get along with after a few dates: 28%
3. Women who get serious too fast: 18%

Women

1. Partners with "baggage": 35%
2. Not enough men, and not knowing how to find them: 23%
3. Men who get serious too fast: 21%

Sex in Society

Americans aren't bashful about their sex lives, if survey responses and reality TV are any indication. So if official census takers had the nerve to ask the right questions, they might blush to learn that:

- The average American has sex 118 times per year—pretty impressive, but a little lower than the worldwide average of 127 times a year.
- Three-quarters of those polled were happy with their sex lives.
- Forty-five percent of people admitted they had experienced a one-night stand.
- Among women, 48 percent admitted that they sometimes fake an orgasm.

When the Internet was first gaining popularity, some futurists predicted that, in a few years, Americans would be doing everything online—and they did mean everything. Not just banking, shopping, and learning, but sex too. Some thought this would be a good thing:

the safest sex, they claimed, would be cyber sex. Partners separated by computer wires, or maybe just one person at a time hooking up with a virtual lover, would become the norm. Others thought that sounded a little boring—not to mention unlikely. It was.

Now that Internet users number in the billions, there certainly are more than a few people who scratch their particular itch virtually. But as it turned out, most people still get their groove on live and in person. So what does the 21st century American sexual profile look like?

Loss of Virginity

For one thing, virginity is apparently just about what it used to be: something the typical American loses before they are old enough to legally drink beer or vote. The average male loses his virginity a little younger, at just under 17, while the average female holds out a few months longer, according to the Guttmacher Institute. Those numbers haven't changed much in a generation. That's despite the fact that 86% of public schools in the country promote sexual abstinence as part of their sex education strategy.

But before parents panic too much, it seems that fewer than half—48 percent—of high school students have ever had sexual intercourse. A few early starters bring down the average age: One of every seven high school students has already had four or more sex partners. Before they reach 20, however, three-quarters of all men and women have had sexual intercourse.

Taking a Position

Traditional, "missionary" position intercourse is still the favorite, with 79% of all sex being done with the woman laying face up with her male partner atop. The second most popular missionary position is with the woman atop, comprising about one-third of all missionary style sex. In second place overall is "doggy style" at 31%.

Favorite Sex Toy

In 2009, just under 50% of respondents reported using a vibrator at some point, with slightly more women (52%) than men (45%) reporting vibrator use. Women reported using vibrators most during masturbation (46%) and least during intercourse (37%). Men were most likely to use vibrators with a partner during "sex play or foreplay" (40%). Only 17% of men reported using a vibrator for masturbation. Forty percent of men said they used one to help a partner with orgasms, and 7% said they used it to help themselves have an orgasm.

Where We Put It

Nine out of 10 Americans report having had sex of some kind during the past year. The vast majority of those sexual experiences were vaginal intercourse. But more than a fourth of men, and 19 percent of women, have given or received oral sex. Anal sex is not quite as common: Only about one in 10 people say they have had anal sex in the past year, although a third of Americans have tried it at least once in their life.

Sexual Orientation

Not all of that hanky panky is between heterosexual partners. The National Center for Health Statistics estimates that nearly 5 million Americans consider themselves either bisexual or homosexual. Here's a summary of sexual orientation among Americans (the totals don't add up to 100% due to self-reported findings from varying studies):

Sexual Orientation	How Many?
Heterosexual	97%
Homosexual	2.8% males, 1.4% females
Bisexual	1.5%

Other Key Facts

Transsexuals in the United States	0.25 to 1%

U.S. men who are cross-dressers	1%
Men who have had same-sex relations	6%
Women who have had same-sex relations	10%

Sources: National Center for Health Statistics, American Journal of Psychiatry, *National Health and Social Life Survey,* Self-Help *magazine*

What We Catch

According to the Centers for Disease Control, several hundred thousand Americans contract a sexually transmitted illness every year. The most common: chlamydia, which affected more than 1.2 million people in the U.S. in 2008, most of them women. Gonorrhea was second, with more than 330,000 cases. Syphilis, which can be deadly if not treated, affects about 12,000 Americans each year. Although new cases of HIV in the U.S. have declined in recent years, the CDC estimates that more than 1 million people in the country are infected, and another half million are living with AIDS.

Online Porn

The website Online MBA has collected some mind-blowing stats about the widespread availability and popularity of pornography on the Internet:

- 25 million websites are pornographic—that's 12 percent of the Internet.
- People spend about $3,000 per second on online porn.
- Each year, the online porn industry earns nearly $3 billion
- 2.5 billion pornographic e-mails are sent every day.
- The least popular day of the year for looking at online porn: Thanksgiving.
- The most popular day of the week for looking at online porn: Sunday!

American Family Profiles

For fans of a hit TV series from the 1950s and early 1960s, June and Ward Cleaver were beloved symbols of an American family ideal—even if it was a little too good to be true.

The Cleavers were the fictional parents of Beaver and Wally in *Leave It to Beaver*. The death of actress Barbara Billingsley (June Cleaver) in 2010, nearly 30 years after the passing of Hugh Beaumont (Ward), caused more than a few Americans of a certain age to recall that bygone era in TV and real-world family life. The contrast with current family life may cause a few of them to scratch their heads and wonder what happened.

Describing the typical American family in the early 21st century is about as easy as nailing Jell-O to the wall. In addition to many traditional (or nuclear) families, there are dozens of nontraditional family groupings. They include the 13 million one-parent U.S. households headed by either a mother or a father. They also include many families headed by same-sex couples, childless families, and quasi-family households of cohabiting adults—once derided as "shacking up" but now widely accepted and increasingly common. And many Americans are doing just fine living alone, thank you very much.

Who Is Living with Whom?

The latest data (2009) from the Census Bureau's Current Population Survey, part of the report *America's Families and Living Arrangements,* offers a mild surprise: Nearly 26 million married couples maintain households together with children under 18 at home. It may not be a Ward and June Cleaver existence anymore, but these are traditional households. In fact, there are more than five million "stay-at-home" parents, once the norm in post-World War II America. Nearly all such parents are still mothers, but there are 158,000 stay-at-home fathers.

American Children in Two-Parent Households by Race and Origin

Children	How many
Asian	85%
White, non-Hispanic	78%
Hispanic	69%
Black	38%

Source: America's Families and Living Arrangements

Approximately 7.5 million opposite-sex couples live together, according to 2010 Census Bureau estimates. And there are more than 770,000 same-sex couples in the nation, according to the UCLA School of Law's Williams Institute on Sexual Orientation Law and Public Policy. It's not clear how many of them live together.

Interracial marriage is still the exception, but it's increasingly more frequent. Of all married couples in the country in 2008, a record 14.6% were between spouses of different races or ethnicity. And that doesn't include couples in which both spouses were multiracial.

Now, fewer people get married at all, continuing a half-century decline. According to the 2008 American Community Survey, only 52%

of males 15 and older, and only 48% of females 15 and older, are now married.

It doesn't always last, either. The National Center for Health Statistics found that more than 19% of both men and women saw their first marriages end in separation, divorce, or annulment after five years of marriage. After 10 years, the percentage that end is more than 25% for both sexes.

States with Youngest Median Age, First Marriage

Utah	24
Idaho	24
Arkansas	24
Oklahoma	24

States with Highest Median Age, First Marriage

Connecticut	28
Massachusetts	28
New York	28
Rhode Island	28

Multigenerational Families Make a Comeback

According to the Pew Research Center, one type of family common in earlier American history is back in favor: multigenerational families. The reason, according to Pew, is a combination of economic stresses and increased populations of recent Latin American and Asian immigrants, in which multigenerational households may be more socially acceptable.

As of 2008, nearly 50 million Americans were living in a household with least two adult generations, or a grandparent and someone from at least one other generation. That's 16% of the population, up from 12% in 1980. But there's a long way to go before reaching the level before World War II, when one-quarter of Americans lived in such a family arrangement.

Of those multigenerational households, 47% are two adult generations from the same family. Another 47% have three or more generations, and the remaining skip a generation: A grandchild lives with a grandparent instead of a parent, for example.

One factor adding slightly to the multigenerational family trend is older ages for first marriages. Anyone who has been to a wedding or two lately can attest to the fact that Americans are waiting longer to get hitched. A man's first marriage is now on average just over age 28, while women are nearly 26 at their first marriage. Before they set up house, they sometimes save another year or two of rent money by staying with Mom and Dad.

In addition, a 2009 Pew survey found that one of every eight adults 22 to 29 claimed to have returned home to live with parents due to unemployment or other effects of the economic recession. Those who leave and then move back home have acquired their own wry label: boomerang children.

Another survey found that, despite the long-term trend toward retirement-facility living, more than half of Americans now accept as a "family responsibility" taking into their home an elderly parent.

Living Single

Pew also showed that living alone is more common now than ever before. Now, more than 10% of Americans live in single-person households, compared to just 1.1% in 1900.

Taking Care of Business

What Americans Earn, Learn, and Give

Incomes and Jobs

Most people who read about the early history of the United States know that the nation's founders championed the right to life, liberty, and the pursuit of happiness. That's true, but it's not all that their vision produced. They also helped make it possible for modern Americans to seek the best job they could find, work hard and succeed at it, and reserve the right to complain about their job to their friends. It's a cherished part of the American way!

American writer and humorist Mark Twain saw this coming. Work, he once said, is a necessary evil to be avoided. It's an amusing line, but most people who heard him repeat it also knew that Twain was a prolific writer well acquainted with hard work. Then there's comedian Drew Carey's line: "Oh, you hate your job? Why didn't you say so? There's a support group for that. It's called EVERYBODY, and they meet at the bar."

In a better mood, Twain also said, "*Work* and *play* are words used to describe the same thing under differing conditions." In truth, most people don't appear to hate their jobs, but they worry somewhat about how long it will last.

So what's the condition of America's workplace a decade into the 21st century? The answer may depend on who you ask and when. Just as President Harry Truman once quipped that "it's a recession when your neighbor loses his job; it's a depression when you lose yours," the recession of 2008–09 caused some people to wonder if high unemployment would become the new "normal." Based on U.S. history and most economic projections, that seems unlikely.

In late 2010, the U.S. Bureau of Labor Statistics (BLS) calculated the nationwide unemployment rate at 9.6%, or just under 15 million Americans. Earlier in the year, the rate had declined slightly due in part to temporary jobs for people working on the 2010 U.S. Census. Unemployment was highest, as usual, among teenagers (26%) and African Americans (16.1%). Hispanics (12.4%) also were affected disproportionately by unemployment in 2010.

Of course, the glass is far more than half full if more than 90% of workers have a job. That means that, as of late 2010, nearly 140 million Americans 16 years and older were employed.

The average workweek for American employees was just over 34 hours in late 2010. Those in manufacturing jobs worked longer—just over 40 hours—and factory workers put in an average of three hours of overtime per week.

What Americans Earn

The latest full-year Census Bureau figures (2009) show that the median household income in the country in 2009 was slightly less than $50,000. Other highlights of the annual report *Income, Poverty, and Health Insurance Coverage in the United States: 2009* included:

- Asian households boasted the highest median income.
- Households in the West and Northeast had the highest incomes.
- Women who worked full-time still earned only 77% of what men earned in corresponding jobs.

- The poverty rate was the highest since 1994, at 14.3%. That's more than 43 million people.
- The number of people in poverty in 2009 was the largest since the number was first tracked in 1959.

Jobs in the Future

In addition to reporting short-term workforce dynamics, the BLS also projects future employment trends. The most recent projections, which run through 2018, envision the addition of more than 15 million jobs over a decade. The American workforce, the report says, will be older and more diverse, and job growth will be fastest in service industries.

In fact, more than half of all new jobs are expected to be in professional and related occupations and in service occupations. The civilian labor force is projected to reach nearly 167 million people by 2018, but it will grow more slowly than in the previous decade. Baby Boomers are expected to work to an older age, so the percentage of workers 55 and older is expected to increase by 12 million people, a dramatic rise of 43%.

Although whites will remain the largest race group in the labor force, at nearly 80%, the number of Asians in the labor force could rise by nearly 30%—and African Americans by 14%. The number of Hispanics in the labor force will grow more than one-third.

Where the Jobs Will Be

The BLS expects that three industries will show the most job growth: management, scientific, and technical consulting; computer systems design; and employment services. Those three fields are projected to add more than 2 million jobs.

Other types of work that will see greater demand include those in physicians' offices, home health care, services for the elderly and persons with disabilities, and nursing care facilities. The news is not as rosy for department stores, or for manufacturers of semiconductors and motor vehicle parts. The BLS projects that all three sectors will see job losses through 2018.

Regarding specific jobs, tremendous job growth is projected among registered nurses (582,000), home health aides (461,000), and customer service representatives (400,000).

Odd Jobs

Each year, CareerBuilder.com conducts a survey on interesting or unusual jobs people have held during their working lives. The results are always entertaining. Among those collected in recent years:

- haunted house actor
- rodeo clown
- fingerprint analyzer
- jelly donut filler
- lifeguard at a nude beach
- elf at Santa's workshop
- hurricane hunter
- kitty litter box decorator
- phone psychic
- stand-in bridesmaid
- urinalysis observer
- artificial inseminator at a zoo
- cat nanny
- donkey trainer
- parachute tester
- taster at a chocolate factory
- undercover vice decoy
- wallpaper peeler
- yawn counter at a sleep clinic

Who says there are no interesting jobs left in America? Participants in the survey weren't asked how helpful it was to include those past work experiences on their résumés.

Creative job opportunities are really nothing new in America, however. A collection of occupations from 1880, published by Ancestry.com, shows that you can never really know which lines of work will survive over the long term.

The 1880 federal census found that one of every five workers at the time was a laborer, often on a farm. Other common jobs at the time included carpenter, blacksmith, miner, and cotton mill worker. Others listed their jobs as saloonkeeper, cattle herder, street sweeper, sandwich man, collector of eggs, and preparer of fruit. Even *outlaw* turned up on some census forms.

Dangerous Jobs and Lucrative Jobs

According to the Bureau of Labor Statistics, fishing industry jobs lead the list of America's most dangerous occupations. The next four in order are logger, pilot and flight engineer, farmer and rancher, and roofer.

Danger doesn't always equate to good pay. According to the BLS, surgeons are the top earners in the country, with an average of nearly $220,000 a year. Other medical jobs that pay an average of more than $200,000 a year include anesthesiologist, oral and maxillofacial surgeon, orthodontist, and obstetrician and gynecologist.

Other job types that make the BLS rankings for earnings above $100,000 a year include lawyer, air traffic controller, and astronomer. Not surprisingly, food service jobs including server, cook, and dishwasher all are near the bottom of the rankings.

Former Jobs of Famous Americans

According to sources including *CNN Living*, *Parade*, and Current.com, some noted Americans worked at humble or strange jobs before they found the niche that made them famous:

- Comedian Chris Rock often jokes about scrambling to make enough money working at Red Lobster to pay for a meal there.
- Actor Bill Murray sold chestnuts.
- Director Quentin Tarantino claims he once was an usher at an adult movie theater.
- Former Secretary of State General Colin Powell worked in a store that sold baby furniture.
- Actor Warren Beatty once had a job catching rats.
- Billionaire Warren Buffett started his road to riches by working in his grandfather's grocery store.
- Actor Matthew McConaughey had a job in Australia that included shoveling chicken manure.
- Singer Gwen Stefani worked at a Dairy Queen.
- Actor Tom Cruise once earned money as a paperboy.
- Actor Brad Pitt earned a few dollars wearing a chicken costume to promote a restaurant.
- Before he was a successful novelist, Stephen King was a teacher.
- President Grover Cleveland was previously an executioner.

Be nice to that young person mopping the floor or bagging your groceries. He or she may become your favorite hip-hop singer—or your future president.

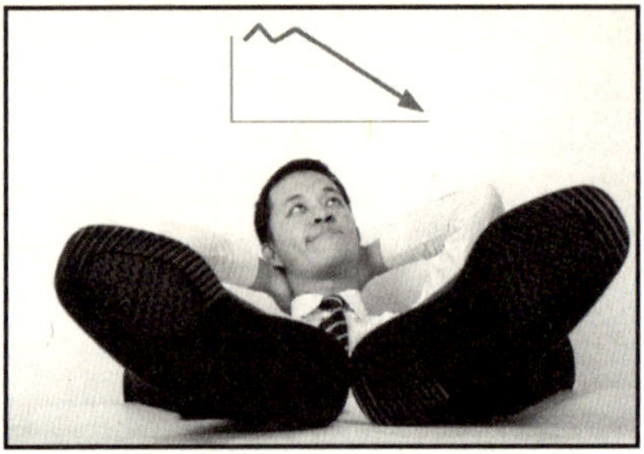

America's Net Worth

Americans have come a long way since the Colonial Era. Back then, the average per-capita net worth was approximately 74 British pounds, which comes out to just over $1,000 in today's money.

Now, according to Federal Reserve statistics in 2010, the average person in the United States is worth $182,000. That may sound unlikely to anyone living from paycheck to paycheck, until you realize that the net worth total includes the assets of not just teachers and firemen, but also of Bill Gates, Warren Buffet, and other successful Americans with extraordinary balance sheets.

The net worth of American households together in mid-2010 was $53.5 trillion, give or take a buck or two. That's the value of every house (and mortgage) and bank account (and credit card balance) as well as stocks, bonds, and other assets and debts.

Despite low interest rates on savings, Americans in 2010 were putting away around 6% of their incomes. That was three times the savings rate of just three years earlier, before the start of a crisis in financial and housing markets that led to an 18-month recession.

Americans had trimmed their total indebtedness from historic highs to $13.5 trillion by the middle of the year, but that's not chiefly because they were paying down balances. Most of the decrease was due to people defaulting on mortgages and other debt. Financial experts expect it will be several years before the personal debt levels of Americans can decline to a more ideal level.

CreditCards.com, which amasses statistics from sources including the Federal Reserve and Fitch Ratings, provided this profile of American credit card use and indebtedness in 2010:

Number	**Credit Card Fact**
$15,788	credit card debt per U.S. household with such debt
609.8 million	number of credit cards held by American consumers
3.5	average number of credit cards per cardholder
$852.6 billion	total U.S. revolving debt (98% is credit card debt)
$2.42 trillion	total U.S. consumer debt (excluding real estate debt)
13.0%	rate of default on U.S. credit cards

And those numbers are just for consumers. They don't account for the average American's share of the $14 trillion of government debt, which works out to about $45,000 per man, woman, and child.

According to the annual *Forbes* list of the 400 richest Americans (in terms of net worth), four of the top 10 are members of the Walton family, heirs to the business and fortune of WalMart founder Sam Walton.

1.	Bill Gates	$54 billion
2.	Warren Buffett	$45 billion
3.	Larry Ellison	$27 billion
4.	Christy Walton	$24 billion
5.	Charles Koch	$21.5 billion
6.	David Koch	$21.5 billion

7. Jim Walton $20.1 billion
8. Alice Walton $20 billion
9. S. Robson Walton $19.7 billion
10. Michael Bloomberg $18 billion

Pols and Celebs Who Roll in Dough

Although few politicians are worth as much money as the top entrepreneurs in the country, elected officials at the national level aren't exactly the family next door, either. The Center for Responsive Politics analyzed the net worth of members of Congress after the 2008 national elections and found that incumbents reelected that November had an average net worth of $815,000. Moreover, newly elected members of Congress were worth more than twice that much: an average of $1.8 million!

A few American celebrities have parlayed their success on stage, screen, or television into big money. These are the big winners, according to *Forbes:*

Celebrity	**Annual Earnings**
Oprah Winfrey	$315 million
Tyler Perry	$125 million
Tiger Woods	$105 million
Steven Spielberg	$100 million
Beyonce Knowles	$87 million

Bruce Springsteen and Howard Stern trailed those five super-earners, but they can't really complain: Both The Boss and the king of shock radio earned $70 million in just 12 months. It's not bad work if you can get it.

For many Americans, especially during a period of soft housing prices and stock market valuations off their highs in 2007, net worth is an ambiguous term. In fact, at one point during the 2008–09 recession, economists calculated that 41 million Americans were living with a net worth of zero. In more than a few cases, that's not because they were unemployed or owned no assets, but because they owed at least as much as their houses and bank accounts were worth.

How much people are worth financially depends in part on where they live in the United States. For most of the past 20 years, the northeastern U.S. has led in average household net worth, according to Federal Reserve statistics. People in the West have generally been a close second and have occasionally edged out their East Coast fellow citizens. Midwestern average net worth has consistently run third among the four regions, and the South has remained fourth.

Wealthy Pets

According to *Reader's Digest,* in 1931 Ella Wendel died and left $30 million to her poodle. That fortune has more than tripled since then, and it's technically the property of poodle Toby Rimes, a descendent of the original lucky dog.

Controversial hotel millionaire Leona Helmsley died in 2007 and willed $12 million in a trust fund to Trouble, her pet Maltese. Although the state later reduced the doggie fund to "only" $2 million, that provided enough capital to keep Trouble in the style to which she was accustomed. Funding for her annual expenses included $1,200 for food, $8,000 for grooming, and $100,000 for 24/7 security. It's a dog's life.

The Things Americans Own

In the 1979 comedy film *The Jerk,* Steve Martin plays Navin Johnson, a likeable dolt who makes and loses a fortune on an ill-conceived invention. He also gains, loses, and then regains love. In one hilarious scene, Navin the ruined entrepreneur walks out on his woman, his home, and most of his possessions. He exclaims, "I don't need anything except this…ashtray. And this paddle game…and this remote control. The ashtray, the paddle game, and the remote control, and that's all I need."

Before leaving, Navin adds a pack of matches and a lamp to his armload. Later, a homeless Navin trades it all for a thermos. Ridiculous? Yes, in a funny Steve Martin way. But many Americans watching that "I don't need anything" scene may have felt something uncomfortably familiar about the idea that we can't live without our stuff.

Another American funny man, George Carlin, poked fun at himself and his audience with an extended monologue that included the line, "That's all you need in life: a little place for your stuff."

One of the first things you learn about ownership statistics is that in a country as big as America, with 310 million consumers all buying, selling, trading, donating, and losing things, nobody really knows who owns what stuff, or where they keep it. But Americans own a lot of stuff, and here's a partial list.

Houses. The American Dream, owning a home, has experienced some ups and down in the past decade. But despite a boom in housing values, followed by a bust and a scary period of mortgage defaults and foreclosures, the homeownership rate in the U.S. remains just under 67%. That often-quoted government statistic doesn't mean that two-thirds of Americans own a home. It means that two-thirds of the occupied housing units in the nation are occupied by the owner. So out of the more than 112 million occupied housing units in the country, 75 million of them provide a roof over the head of their owners. Despite the worrisome news in recent years, it's worth noting that the homeownership rate was lower in 1985 (64%).

Solar panels. Solar energy advocates claim that 1.5 million Americans use solar power to heat water for homes or swimming pools. Solar Developments, an equipment provider, estimates that 200,000 homes in the U.S. have some kind of solar panel technology. Of those, roughly 5%, or 10,000 homes, are said to be entirely powered by solar energy.

Pools and hot tubs. Americans own a lot of swimming pools and hot tubs. Key facts according to the Association of Pool and Spa Professionals:

5.8 million	Hot tubs in the U.S.
4.6 million	In-ground pools
4.1 million	Above-ground pools

Top 5 Pool-Owning States

	State	Pools
1.	California	1.4 million
2.	Florida	845,000
3.	Texas	709,000
4.	New York	450,000
5.	Ohio	355,000

Source: APSP

Barbecue grills. There may not be a pool in every backyard, but there's a barbecue grill in most of them. According to the Hearth, Patio & Barbecue Association, 82% of all U.S. households have a grill or smoker. Those who own grills give them a workout; 97% of grill owners use them.

Microwave ovens. The microwave was discovered in 1945 when a radar engineer accidentally melted a chocolate bar in his pocket during an experiment. By 1975, there were a million microwave ovens in American homes. Now, according to the Bureau of Labor Statistics, more than 90% of American homes have food-nuking capability.

Dishwashers. After Americans zap their dinner in the microwave and finish eating, most of them can put the dirty dishes in an automatic dishwasher instead of rolling up their sleeves at the sink. The Consortium for Energy Efficiency estimates that just over 60% of American homes contain a dishwasher.

Televisions. A recent Nielsen's Television Audience Report revealed that nearly 115 million American homes have at least one television. But that's not the whole story. The average home had nearly three TVs in 2009, an increase of 18% in just one decade. The next time you hear a TV on somewhere in the house, consider this: There are more TVs

(2.86) than people (2.5) in the average home. Nielsen also estimates that 88% of U.S. homes have a DVD player. The era of the VCR is clearly fading, but 72% of U.S. homes still have one that erupted, just in case somebody wants to see the video of the family food fight last Thanksgiving.

Musical instruments. A Gallup survey found that 51% of U.S. households own at least one musical instrument.

Computers and other technology. A 2010 report revealed the extraordinary adoption of computers and other personal technology devices by Americans in the early 21st century. Researchers from the Pew Internet & American Life Project looked at what they called the "key appliances of the information age." Here's what they found:

Cell phones: Eighty-five percent of Americans 18 and older own one. Among people 18 to 29, the rate is nearly 100%. These days, cell phones are so ubiquitous that no one would bat an eye if a great-grandmother used her cell phone to call her great-granddaughter. Cell phones are likely to remain the "gadget of choice" for years to come.

Computers: Seventy-six percent of American adults now own a computer. The PC is increasingly portable; laptop ownership rose from 30% to 52% in just four years.

MP3 players: Nearly half of adults own an iPod or other portable device dedicated to playing MP3 audio files. It's easy to overlook how fast the MP3 industry blossomed. Only 11% of American adults owned one five years ago.

Game consoles: About half of American adults have a PlayStation, Xbox, or other console video game device. Many others play video games via their computers or handheld digital devices.

Electronic readers: Pew's study noted the nascent phase of what it expects to be a booming market among Americans for e-readers such as the Kindle, Nook, Reader, and other competitors. Only one in 20 adults now owns one of the devices, but the number is expected to grow rapidly with the introduction of more durable, lower-priced units.

Guns. The National Rifle Association, Brady Center, and other groups estimate that more than 70 million Americans own at least one firearm. There are at least 300 million privately owned firearms in the country, a third of them handguns.

Cars. A 2006 Nielsen research study found that 190 million Americans own a motor vehicle.

Bicycles. It's impossible to know exactly how many bikes are out there, since many are hanging on a wall in a shed or rusting on a bike rack. The advocacy group Rails to Trails claims that more than 100 million Americans own bicycles.

Stocks or bonds. In 2010, the *New York Times* estimated that half of Americans—more than 150 million—owned stock in one form or another. Most of them owned stock through mutual funds and other investment vehicles rather than buying specific numbers of shares in individual companies.

401(k) accounts. A Harris poll found that 45% of American workers participate in a 401(k) or 403(b) retirement plan through their place of employment. Another 14% of workers choose not to participate, and 35% have jobs that don't offer that type of retirement savings account.

Animals. The 2009–10 National Pet Owners Survey found that nearly two-thirds of American households own at least one pet. The American Pet Products Association estimates that 3.9 million households own a horse. Half of them buy gifts for their horses.

Tigers and snakes. The Humane Society says that nearly 40% of households own at least one dog, and one-third own at least one cat. Some of the 71 million pet-owning homes in the nation have something more exotic than a cat or a dog. An expert at the St. Louis Zoo estimates that as many as 10,000 tigers are kept as private pets, a population that dwarfs the 400 tigers cared for in American zoos. The American Veterinary Medical Association estimates that 390,000 U.S. households own a snake.

Fish. Millions of Americans maintain home aquariums and keep either freshwater or saltwater fish. A small, unknown number of Americans keep piranha fish. But the voracious fish are outlawed as pets in 24 states, including nearly all southern states. Piranhas that are dumped illegally into the wild could possibly survive and become a danger to humans and other species.

Islands. If you're really bored with owning houses, gadgets, and snakes, you might consider buying an island. *Private Island Magazine,* which covers the island-buying lifestyles of the rich and famous, says American celebrities who have bought islands include country music singers Faith Hill and Tim McGraw and actors Eddie Murphy, Brooke Shields, Leonardo DiCaprio, Johnny Depp, and Mel Gibson.

Getting to Work

Americans who commute to jobs in the city know that the 9 to 5 workday is a myth. That's because, in order to arrive at work on time, many of them get up long before dawn to get in a long line on the freeway or find a seat on the early train.

According to the U.S. Bureau of Transportation Statistics, the average driver in the country covers 29 miles each day and is in the car for about 55 minutes. That doesn't sound too bad, does it? No, but it includes millions of people in smaller cities and many others who use their cars for something other than commuting.

The real pain of commuting can be found in the U.S. Department of Housing and Urban Development's American Housing Survey. The 2008 edition discovered that more than 17 million people—13% of all commuters—leave home for work between midnight and 5:59 A.M. And *you* think it's cruel when your alarm clock goes off at 6:30!

Some of those early riders may have early shifts, but others are trying to beat the crush they know will develop on the freeways later in the morning. Many people just have a long way to travel: A staggering 3.5

million Americans experience an average daily commute of at least 90 minutes—one way.

Not surprising to those who have experienced rush-hour traffic around New York City or Washington, D.C., those commuters are the big-city endurance champions, according to HUD.

Longest Average Commuting Times

New York	31.6 minutes
Maryland	31.5 minutes
All U.S. commuters	25.5 minutes

On the other extreme, *Money* magazine's 2009 Best Places database, drawn from census data, found a few American cities with commutes so short that drivers barely have time to find a good radio station.

Shortest Commutes

1. Logan, UT	10.6 minutes
2. Stillwater, OK	10.7 minutes
3. Manhattan, KS	11.1 minutes
4. Grand Forks, ND	11.3 minutes
5. Bismarck, ND	11.8 minutes
6. Dubuque, IA	11.8 minutes
7. Ames, IA	12.0 minutes
8. St. George, UT	12.1 minutes
9. Pocatello, ID	12.1 minutes
10. Lake Havasu City, AZ	12.2 minutes

How We Get to Work

Of the more than 125 million American commuters, the U.S. Department of Housing and Urban Development says that, despite those express lanes for high occupancy vehicles, 76% of people drive to work alone. Only 11% carpool, while 5% take public transportation.

But things could be changing. A 2010 Brookings report found that the percentage of Americans taking mass transit increased from 2000 to 2008, the first rise in that number in four decades.

Biking and Hoofing It

Transportation Alternatives, an advocacy group, was cheered by U.S. Census Bureau research that revealed that nearly 800,000 Americans rode their bikes to work in 2008. That was up by more than 25%, undoubtedly due to a spike in gas prices at the pump. Another 147,000 commuters rode their motorcycles to work.

The two-wheel commuting crowd is just a drop in the proverbial bucket: They make up less than 1% of the total commuters every day. But in some cities, cycling to work gets more respect, according to HUD.

Large U.S. Cities with the Most Bicycle Commuters

1. Portland, OR	3.5%
2. Minneapolis	2.4%
3. Seattle	2.3%
4. Tucson	2.2%
5. San Francisco	1.8%
6. Sacramento	1.8%
7. Washington	1.7%
8. Oakland	1.5%
9. Honolulu	1.4%
10. Denver	1.4%

Among 50 cities studied, Kansas City, Memphis, Indianapolis, Wichita, Omaha, and San Antonio were lowest on the bike-commuting ladder.

Large U.S. Cities with the Most Walking Commuters

Believe it or not, the American Community Survey found that walking (2.5% of commuters) is the fourth most popular mode of commuting.

1. Boston 12.5%
2. Washington 10%
3. San Francisco 9.6%
4. New York 9.4%
5. Philadelphia 8.1%
6. Honolulu 6.9%
7. Seattle 6.9%
8. Minneapolis 5.8%
9. Chicago 5.5%
10. Baltimore 5.4%

But don't expect to see very many people walking to work in Arlington, Texas (0.9%), Fort Worth, Texas (1.1%), or Oklahoma City (1.4%).

The Commuter Pain Index

No one statistic can show how annoying it can be getting to work in a major city. So IBM researchers crunched a variety of measurements, including commuting time, the price of gas, drivers' opinions about how much anger and stress they feel, and even the number of people who just give up on a gridlocked day and stay home from work.

The first global Commuter Pain Index, in 2010, revealed that only three U.S. commutes are among the 20 most painful in the world. On a 100-point scale, Los Angeles commuters register a 25 on the pain index, ahead of New York (19) and Houston (17). But they are practically on Cloud Nine compared to drivers in Beijing and Mexico City, which top the Commuter Pain Index at an agonizing 99!

Educational Attainment

Think about this the next time you're in a room with about 10 people: According to the latest American Community Survey (ACS) numbers, eight of those 10 people have at least a high school diploma. Two or more of them have at least a college degree. One probably has an advanced degree.

America is an educated society. The latest ACS estimates show that nearly 80 million Americans are enrolled in some type of school. Approximately 2.5 million people have taken so many classes that they have a doctorate or equivalent final degree in their field.

Population 3 Years and Older Enrolled in School

Nursery school	5 million
Kindergarten	4 million
Elementary school	16 million
Middle school	16 million
High school	17 million
College (undergraduate)	17 million
Graduate school	3 million

That's a lot of homework, and grading it requires a lot of teachers. The Bureau of Labor Statistics estimates that there are slightly more than 3.5 million teachers educating kindergarteners through high school students.

But some experts believe the U.S. will have to do more in order to remain competitive in the global economy. The National Center for Higher Education Management Systems (NCHEMS) has projected that the country needs 800,000 more college graduates every year until 2025 just to keep up with long-term economic demand. The center estimates that 46% of Americans 25 to 64 have associates degrees or higher, compared with 55% to 60% in some developed nations.

Top 5 U.S. States for College Degrees

1.	Massachusetts	49.6%
2.	Connecticut	46.6%
3.	New Hampshire	46.0%
4.	Colorado	45.3%
5.	North Dakota	45.2%

Source: National Center for Higher Education Management Systems

Knowledge = Earning Power

How much education Americans have translates directly to how much money they earn, according to ACS figures. The median annual income for someone with less than a high school education is just under $20,000. Adding that high school diploma adds $8,000 a year to your bank account. Keep studying until you have at least a bachelor's degree and the money really changes: $47,000 in annual earnings. And Americans with a graduate or professional degree average more than $63,000 a year.

Despite the anxiety that many people feel these days about the economy, knowledge still makes it easier to succeed financially in America. The NCHEMS found that when nationwide unemployment was around 10 percent, only 4.5 percent of college graduates were out of work.

A Charitable Nation

From one end of the economic spectrum to the other, Americans give to charities at a stunning rate. In 2009 alone, they donated more than $300 billion to their favorite causes, according to the Center on Philanthropy at Indiana University. Due to the recession, that was a slight decline from previous years, but the general trend for giving is up, up, and away.

That's an average of nearly $1,000 a year for every single man, woman, and child in the nation, although actual donating behavior ranges from nothing at all to more than $700 million! The $300 billion total came from more than 75 million U.S. households and more than a million companies and other organizations.

Who Gets the Money?

The Center on Philanthropy and the Giving USA Foundation found that religious groups are the biggest beneficiaries of charitable giving, attracting one-third of the money each year. Here's a list of the top beneficiaries in 2009:

1.	Religion	$100 billion
2.	Education	$40 billion
3.	Foundations	$31 billion
4.	Human services	$27 billion
5.	Arts, culture, humanities	$12 billion
6.	International assistance	$9 billion
7.	Environment/animals	$6 billion

Earn More, Give More—Even After We Die

In 2009, people who died left nearly $24 billion to charities. But whether it's a will or a donation by the living, people with higher incomes are more likely to give to charity, according to a Gallup poll.

An earlier Gallup poll revealed that families who earned $20,000 a year or less give approximately $450 to charity each year. Those who earned more than $100,000 donated an average of slightly more than $3,000.

Giving by Income Group

Activity	$75K+	$30K to $74K	Less than $30K
Donate to religious causes	67%	58%	50%
Donate to other causes	87%	76%	59%
Donate blood	15%	18%	12%

The same poll found that men and women give money at about the same rates, although men give blood more often.

Really Big Gifts to Charity

The Giving USA Foundation has found that U.S. households with at least $1 million in wealth give half of all charitable contributions. But as a percentage of income, low-income working families are the most generous group of all, giving approximately 4.5% of their income to good causes—compared to 2.5% for the middle class and 3% for high-income people.

But for the really eye-popping donations, look to the richest people. Stanley Druckenmiller, the CEO at Duquesne Capital, led the way in 2009 by giving more than $700 million through his family's foundation. It gives grants for research in medicine and to support education and poverty initiatives. The Druckenmiller list of donations that year included $100 million toward the cost of building an institute at New York University that will study neuroscience and stem-cell therapy.

The *Chronicle of Philanthropy* recently listed these five biggest charitable donations by wealthy Americans:

1. Stanley & Fiona Druckenmiller, $705 million (medical research, education, poverty)
2. John Templeton, $573 million (various research causes)
3. Bill and Melinda Gates, $350 million (various causes)
4. Michael Bloomberg, $254 million (accident prevention and other causes)
5. Louise Dieterle Nippert, $185 million (cultural causes)

Creative Ways to Give

Leave it to Americans to come up with some truly unusual ways to raise money for charity. Luxury cars from the HBO series *The Sopranos* were auctioned to raise money for a children's hospital and other causes. One Cadillac driven by Carmela Soprano, one of the show's stars, drew a winning bid of $90,000 for the Andre Agassi Charitable Foundation. The New Orleans Saints allotted an NFL championship ring to a nonprofit group, which auctioned the ring to raise money for victims of the destructive BP oil spill in the Gulf of Mexico.

Several college-based organizations have raised money for charity in recent years by having contributors sponsor walk-a-thon participants in heels—men in heels, that is. Utah State and the University of Wisconsin-Milwaukee used that tactic to raise money and attention for programs to prevent sexual assault and domestic violence.

For people who can't get motivated to raise money in heels, here's a creative gadget for giving even before you get out of bed in the morning—especially if you try to catch a few extra winks. The SnuzNLux alarm clock connects to the owner's Internet-based bank account. It makes a donation to charity every time he or she hits the snooze button when the alarm goes off.

The 21st century list of big donations by wealthy business leaders hasn't yet seen anything to rival a 1998 donation of $1 million by Alan Greenberg, former CEO of the investment bank Bear Stearns. Greenberg, who made the pledge long before his firm made mostly negative news during the 2008 financial crisis, got both applause and boos for his donation to pay for Viagra prescriptions for poor men.

Just Weird Ways to Give

In addition to time, money, and blood, Americans also donate hundreds of millions of dollars worth of personal property to Goodwill and other agencies each year. Mostly, they give clothing, furniture, jewelry, cars, music items, and other secondhand goods that can be resold to help fund employment and other social services. But sometimes, the things workers find in the donation box are downright strange.

According to the *Las Vegas Sun*, a Goodwill donation-processing center in Nevada has received numerous dangerous items, including spears, swords, loaded guns, and even a live hand grenade! Associated Press accounts in recent years have covered other strange charitable gifts, including a land mine in Denver, a bag of marijuana, human teeth, and other assorted oddities.

Plugged In

Feeding Our Digital Habit

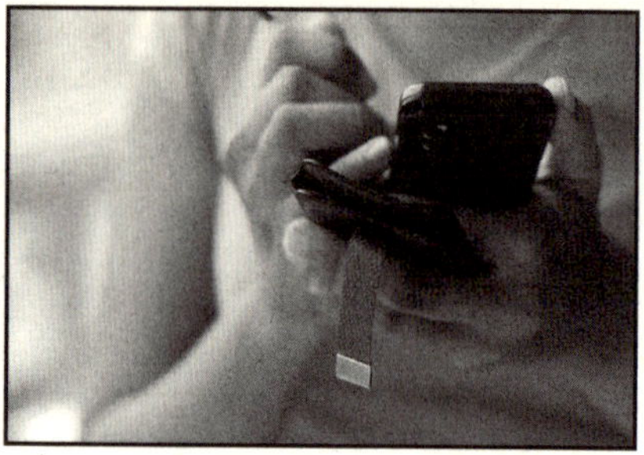

Living Online

A generation ago, there was no such thing as the World Wide Web. No Facebook, Twitter, Google, Yahoo, or any of the other funny names for Internet services most people now take for granted. But now, an amazing number of Americans increasingly are living their lives online. They interact with other people, buy goods and services, learn, communicate, and entertain themselves almost entirely through the illuminated screen of a computer on their desk or lap.

Does that sound like an exaggeration? Consider that a Pew Research Center survey of Americans in 2010 found that:

- 79% of both men and women use the Internet, including a stunning 95% of Americans ages 18 to 29 and a respectable and growing 42% of those 65 and older
- 55% connect to the Internet using a wireless computer or a smart phone such as a BlackBerry or iPhone
- 60% have high-speed Internet connections at home, giving them cheap access to entertainment and other online content

- 67% of rural Americans go online, compared to more than 80% of urban and suburban dwellers

Face Time on Facebook

As of mid-2010, advertising records showed that there were nearly 134 million Americans—and counting—on the social media site Facebook. That's nearly one-third of the more than 500 million Facebook users worldwide. The site now accounts for more than 7% of all Internet visits in the United States, passing the search site Google in 2010 for the first time, according to the Internet research company Hitwise.

Together, all of those people spend more than 700 billion minutes on the site—every month! The average Facebook user has 130 "friends," or contacts on the site, and half of all Facebook users visit the site at least once a day to exchange messages or pictures with others.

InsideFacebook.com estimates that more than 56% of people on Facebook are women, especially young women. But overall, the site attracts a multigenerational audience in the U.S., with roughly half of its audience 35 or older.

Tweeting Is Not Just for the Birds

Twitter, another social media site, lets people share their thoughts and information with others via short messages of no more than 140 characters at a time. In recent years, it has grown as rapidly as Facebook. A 2010 presentation at Chirp, an official Twitter conference, revealed these mind-boggling facts about that growth:

- Twitter has more than 105 million registered users, and it adds more than a quarter-million more every day.
- People send approximately 55 million tweets, or messages, a day.
- More than a third of those people use their cell phones, not a computer, to communicate on Twitter.

Twitter, Facebook, Tumblr, MySpace, and other social media Internet sites increasingly play a role in communicating more than just what friends are having for lunch. News and images of the spectacular water landing on the Hudson of a US Airways passenger jet in 2009 broke first on Twitter, not in the *New York Times* or on CNN.

Second Life and Other Virtual Worlds

The virtual world is another type of online socializing that has had its ups and downs but still engages millions of Americans. Second Life is a program that lets adults 18 and older create avatars to represent themselves and then roam around an online world, known as the "grid." There, they can socialize, trade goods and services, and hold meetings. Second Life had more than 800,000 registered users in early 2010 according to Linden Lab, the company that created and operates Second Life. Teen Second Life was created for 13- to 17-year-olds.

For people who enjoy video games, the Internet has attracted millions of people to online role-playing games such as World of Warcraft. WoW, as it is sometimes called, claimed to have more than 11 million monthly subscribers as of late 2008.

Other Ways of Living Online

Americans now routinely conduct parts of their lives online that previously had nothing to do with computers (much less the Internet) a generation ago, including education, banking, travel, and entertainment. As of late 2010, Pew Research provided this profile of just a few ways that Americans used the Internet in addition to e-mailing or using a search engine:

43% Get news
34% Check the weather
26% Do their banking
23% Watch a video on a video-sharing site like YouTube or Google Video

19% Look online for news or information about politics
16% Research for school or training
15% Get sports scores and info
12% Get financial info, such as stock quotes or mortgage interest rates
10% Search for a map or driving directions
8% Buy a product
7% Pay their bills
7% Look up a phone number or address
5% Look for religious/spiritual info
5% Buy or make a reservation for travel
4% Participate in an online auction
2% Use an online dating website
2% Make a phone call
1% Take a class for credit toward a degree of some kind
1% Make a donation to a charity

With the U.S. population close to 310 million, you can do a little math and see that some parts of the Internet are already far more "populous" than the big cities where so many people live their traditional, 3-D lives.

What We Google

Once upon a time, Americans searched for information by leafing through the pages of a telephone directory, encyclopedia, dictionary, or other book. In the 21st century, that sometimes still happens, but it's rapidly becoming the exception.

Internet searching rules the day. A Nielsen report in 2010 estimated that U.S. Internet search companies handled more than 9 billion searches *a month* by people at home or at work. That's pretty amazing when you consider that the World Wide Web didn't even exist 30 years ago.

Leading U.S. Internet Search Sites, August 2010

Search Site	Searches	Market Share
1. Google	6 billion	65%
2. MSN/Windows/Bing	1.3 billion	14%
3. Yahoo!	1.2 billion	13%
4. Ask.com	197 million	2.1%
5. AOL	180 million	2%

In 2001, people began to shorten "I'm going to search for that on Google" to "I'll Google it," according to *Merriam-Webster* dictionary experts. By the mid-2000s, both *Merriam-Webster* and the *Oxford English Dictionary* had added *Google* as a verb.

What Are We Googling?

What are we looking up on Google and other search engines? Addresses, phone numbers, history facts, how-to lessons, entertainment news, health facts, and occupational advice are part of the search story. Oh, and how to kiss, what to name the baby, and which celebrity died or pled not guilty.

Google's public research team recently published a list of the top 80 most common online searches in 2009 for information that can be found on government or international websites.

Most Common Google Searches for Public Data

1. School comparisons
2. Unemployment
3. Population
4. Sales taxes
5. Salaries
6. Exchange rates
7. Crime
8. Health conditions
9. Disasters
10. Gross Domestic Product

Other topics on the list included income, cancer, marriage, divorce, food prices, first names, weather, and more. But for a peek into the inquiring minds of Americans and worldwide Internet searchers, and how they have changed over the past decade, Google's Zeitgeist reports tell more.

In 2001, according to Google, the five hottest search topics by the end of the year—shortly after the terrorist attacks in New York, Washington, and Pennsylvania—were Nostradamus, CNN, World Trade Center, Harry Potter, and Anthrax. By that time, online surfers were losing interest in the Olympics, the 2000 U.S. elections, and Pokémon.

Top searches that year for women included Britney Spears, Pamela Anderson, and Madonna. Men of interest included Nostradamus (who had been dead for centuries but whose predictions fascinated many), Osama Bin Laden, and Michael Jackson. Top 2001 movies searched on Google included *Harry Potter, Lord of the Rings,* and *Shrek.* As for music, the Beatles still led the search results, followed closely by U2 and 'N Sync. Regarding television, *Big Brother* and *The Simpsons* were in the mix.

By the end of the decade, however, few of those people and topics were still on the minds of American Google searchers, according to the 2009 Google Zeitgeist report. One exception: Michael Jackson's death caused a surge in a search of his name. In fact, it brought major news and search websites to their knees for several hours in June 2009.

Searching for Fame

A decade after Britney, Pam, and Madonna were much searched-after, contemporary stars of interest include pop stars and athletes who are known for their messages, or "tweets," on Twitter. Miley Cyrus, Lance Armstrong, Taylor Swift, Ashton Kutcher, and Shaquille O'Neal have millions of followers who hang on their every tweet.

If searches for concert tickets are any guide, Taylor Swift, the Jonas Brothers, and U2 are among the hottest performers in recent years.

Recently departed famous Americans searched for most often online include Michael Jackson, infomercial pitchman Billy Mays, Farrah Fawcett, Patrick Swayze, and Walter Cronkite. People are very interested in the real or rumored breakups of famous people, including reality stars Jon and Kate Gosselin (true), politician Sarah and husband Todd Palin (rumor), and wrestler Hulk and wife Linda Hogan (true).

In 2010, the expensive divorce of Tiger Woods and Elin Nordegren heated up the computer servers at more than one Internet firm. Celebrity marriages that led the search parade included those of NFL quarterback Tom Brady, *Playboy* celebrity Kendra Wilkinson, tennis player Andy Roddick, and others.

Americans also search for exercise information online, including Pilates, yoga, strength conditioning, and Zumba, with a few "exercise" curiosities mixed in such as hula-hoops and pole dancing. Top Googled diets in recent years included South Beach, Atkins, Acai berry, Mediterranean, and the amazingly popular lemonade diet, a detoxifying juice fast.

Learning to Kiss, Fight, and Crochet?

Americans increasingly use the Internet for both formal education and basic how-to advice. Top searches include:

1. Kiss
2. Draw
3. Knit
4. Crochet
5. Flirt
6. Meditate
7. Hack
8. Sing
9. Dance
10. Fight

By the end of the decade, the top movies by Google searches focused on aliens, vampires, and robots: *Avatar, Twilight,* and *Transformers.* Television shows topping the search ranks included *Glee, Bones,* and *Fringe.*

What are you searching for today?

Phone Facts

Alexander Graham Bell knew he had something good when he patented his telephone invention in 1875. But he couldn't have imagined that, a little more than a century later, people would be carrying around pint-size versions of his invention in their pockets and using them not just to call other people, but also to take photographs, watch movies, and read maps.

And if the 20th century was the heyday of the landline telephone, the 21st century is rapidly becoming the era when Americans are cutting the cord and using smart, mobile devices as their primary, often only, telephones.

In 1919, AT&T installed its first dial telephones in Norfolk, Virginia. For the first time, people could reach someone by dialing the number themselves, rather than picking up the receiver and asking a live operator to connect the call. Amazingly, there were still a few non-dial phones in the country as late as 1978.

That was then, but the future is now. There are more than 285 million subscribers to cell phones in the United States, according to a study by the Cellular Telecommunications and Internet Association (CTIA).

How We Use Cell Phones

Sometime in May 2009, a statistical milestone quietly passed in the history of the telephone: For the first time, there were more American homes (20%) using only a cell phone than the number (17%) using only a landline phone. And there's no turning back the trend.

If you consider all Americans within a household, nearly one-quarter of individuals no longer use a landline telephone at all, according to a National Health Interview Survey. The trend is accelerating, with more than 8% of homes dropping their landline phone each year. Another 15% of people in the country still have a traditional telephone line, but they make or receive nearly all of their phone calls on their cell phones, not on the home phone. In many cases, people keep that extra phone line only for emergencies, or for use as part of a security alarm system or other service unrelated to calling a friend or relative.

At this rate, experts say, traditional phone lines in homes will nearly disappear by 2015. That dizzying downward spiral is no surprise to anyone who witnessed the vanishing of another former American icon: the pay telephone. According to industry sources, there are now approximately 1 million pay phones in the United States, but the total number dropped by more than half from 2007 to 2008, according to the Federal Communications Commission. That's not a coincidence: Former pay phone leader AT&T dropped out of the pay phone business in 2008. Now, the remaining demand is filled by independent companies, who operate almost half of all pay phones.

As cell phones have become common, the once-common need to keep change in your pocket for an emergency call at a phone booth has languished. Still, the American Public Communications Council says there are 1.7 billion calls a year from pay phones, so don't expect to see them go away just yet.

Where the Wireless Things Are

The NHIS found that whether Americans go wireless-only depends somewhat on their age, education level, and region:

Group	% Living in Wireless-Only Households
Midwestern adults	25.6%
Southern adults	25.4%
Western adults	22.2%
Northeastern adults	15.1%
Hispanics	30.4%
Non-Hispanic whites	21%
Non-Hispanic blacks	25%
All men	24.5%
All women	21.3%
College graduates	19.7%
High school graduates	14.2%
No high school diploma	11.5%

The raw number of cell phone users doesn't tell the whole story. To understand the seismic shift underway in telephone use, you have to look at how people are using those wireless wonders.

Pew Internet researchers found that in 2010 nearly a quarter of all cell phone users were actively using smart phone applications, or "apps," in addition to making phone calls and sending text messages. The leading apps, Pew found, are games, news and weather information services, maps, and activity on social networking sites such as Facebook and Twitter.

CTIA, a wireless communications industry association, said in early 2010 that Americans sent or received more than 1.5 trillion text messages a year. The text-me habit shows no sign of slowing down: More than 5 billion messages a day fly through the wireless world. Their content, once more likely to contain social chatter among young cell phone users, now may include everything from emergency-notification alerts from government agencies or schools; bank account alerts; or confirmation of your order for a large pizza with extra cheese and pepperoni.

Conventional text messages, which use the short message service (SMS) technology, may be fun, but they are usually limited to 160 characters per text message. Once people had discovered the benefits of taking photographs and listening to music on their wireless phones, they wanted more options. It was only a matter of time until they started sending their multimedia content to other people. In the second half of 2009, according to CTIA, Americans transmitted more than 24 billion multimedia messaging service (MMS) messages—nearly three times the number of MMS messages sent the previous year.

Pretty soon, we'll want to actually send the pizza itself over the cell phone. No word on whether inventors have solved that one yet, but don't count them out.

Other gee-whiz facts from the CTIA include:

Wireless Phone Facts	2009	2000
Americans w/wireless phone access	91%	69%
Jobs in the wireless industry	250,000	184,000
Wireless industry revenues	$152 billion	$45 billion
Minutes of wireless use by Americans	2.3 trillion	259 billion

Our Video Game Habits

A decade-old Gary Larson cartoon shows two parents watching their video game-obsessed son and dreaming that someday "game player" would be a lucrative profession. Today, that's still funnier than likely. But the way video games have taken America by storm, it makes you wonder what the future may bring.

According to an Entertainment Software Association (ESA) report entitled *2010 Essential Facts About the Computer and Video Game Industry,* more than two-thirds of all U.S. households now play computer or video games. And although 60 percent of players are male, the fastest-growing segment of the gamer population is women over 18. Believe it or not, adult women in the U.S. comprise more of the game-playing market (33%) than boys 17 and younger (20%).

Other key facts from the report:

- The average player of computer or other video games is 34, and he or she started playing 12 years ago.

- More than 40% of heads of households play some type of game on a cell phone or other handheld device.
- More than a quarter of players are over 50. The ESA probably can't wait for more retirement homes to hook up their PlayStations, Wiis, and Xbox 360s for senior gamers!

What Parents Think About Video Games

The ESA estimates that more than three-fourths of parents like the fact that modern video game consoles include options for regulating their kids' access to violent or suggestive game content. In fact, nearly two-thirds of parents now think high-tech games are a good thing for their children, and more than nine in 10 parents claim they personally monitor the purchase or rental of video games by their children.

That's quite a shift from once-common beliefs that digital games were creating little monsters at the other end of the joystick. Maybe enough people by now have watched seemingly hard-wired gamer kids grow up to be normal, productive young adults. Or maybe all of those video gamers in the 50-and-older crowd are just rationalizing.

Whatever the reason, entertainment software is nearly a $5 billion industry in the U.S. And from 2005 to 2009, the industry grew five times faster than the overall American economy. The industry employs more than 120,000 people.

Top States for Video Game Industry Jobs

1. California (41% of all jobs in the industry)
2. Texas
3. Washington
4. New York
5. Massachusetts

To help fill those jobs, more than 500 colleges and other educational institutions worldwide now teach video game development.

Living and Dying

From Homeopathy to Homicide

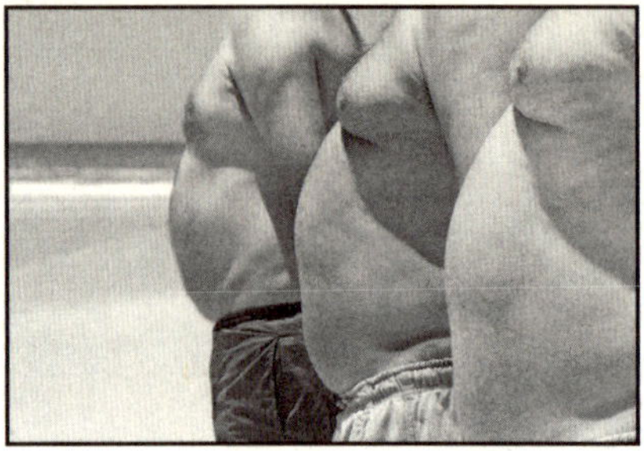

Height and Weight of Americans

The average American man stands halfway between tiny Verne Troyer and towering Igor Vovkovinskiy. Troyer, who played the diminutive Mini-Me in the Austin Powers films, is 2'8" as the result of a type of dwarfism. Vovkovinskiy, a business school student in Minnesota who is a native of Ukraine, was recently confirmed by the *Guinness Book of World Records* as the tallest living American at 7'8.33" tall. Igor is just a third of an inch taller than the second-tallest American, sheriff's deputy George Bell of Virginia.

For most of us, height doesn't dominate our lives, but it may play a role in financial success. Malcolm Gladwell, author of *Blink,* discovered that most chief executive officers of Fortune 500 companies are tall men. The average CEO, he found, is three inches taller than average. Despite what your mother said about height not necessarily making "might," college management researchers estimate that an American earns nearly $800 a year more for every additional inch in height.

The Internet site CelebHeights.com uses a variety of sources to estimate the height of some of Hollywood's leading men.

Tall (or Short) and Handsome

Danny Devito	5'0"
Michael J. Fox	5'4"
Al Pacino	5'5"
Jason Alexander	5'5"
Tom Cruise	5'7"
Sylvester Stallone	5'7"
Robert Downey Jr.	5'7"
Mel Gibson	5'9"
Keanu Reeves	6'1"
Pierce Brosnan	6'2"
Will Smith	6'2"
Danny Glover	6'3"
Clint Eastwood	6'4"
Liam Neeson	6'4"

Data from the U.S. Department of Health and Human Services shows that the average U.S. male is 5'9" and weighs 191 pounds. The average woman: 5'4" and 164 pounds. In 1960, both men and women were an inch shorter and more than 25 pounds lighter. Anyone who has seen vintage clothing or uniforms in a museum exhibit of 19th century artifacts may suspect that better nutrition, health care, and other living standards in modern times have helped people grow taller—and heavier. The problem, according to health researchers, is that modern Americans have become too sedentary and too fond of eating.

Is Overweight the New "Normal"?

A 2010 Harris survey found that American men and women aren't sure how their weight compares to population norms. Nearly one-third who are overweight by Body Mass Index, a combination of weight and height, call themselves "normal" in size. In addition, 70 percent of clinically obese people surveyed call themselves just "overweight."

Most in both groups are more likely to believe that lack of exercise is the culprit when it comes to their weight: 75% of obese people say they don't exercise enough; only 48% say they eat too much. Many experts say that both factors, along with heredity, matter.

Obesity Facts

34% Americans 20 and older who are obese

34% Adults 20 and older who are overweight but not obese

18% Children 12–19 who are obese

20% Children 6–11 who are obese

Source: National Center for Health Statistics

CDC studies of Americans reveal that adult obesity can vary significantly from state to state. More than one-third of Mississippi residents are obese, compared to under 19% of Colorado residents. But the country's weight problem is apparent everywhere: Not a single U.S. state meets the CDC goal of no more than a 15% obesity rate.

The challenge for Americans is not just a matter of perception or self-esteem, of course. According to the CDC, annual U.S. medical costs attributed to obesity are nearly $150 billion. And recent trends are not encouraging. From 2007 through 2009, an additional 2.4 million American adults became obese. Obesity rates are especially high among non-Hispanic black women (41.9%) and Hispanics (30.7%).

To Enter This Ride, You Must Be This Tall

For every kid who grew up marking the latest height on a door frame each year, wondering whether he or she would ever be tall enough to get on the roller coaster ride or make the basketball team, here's a collection of height standards in American life:

One small step for a man: For NASA engineers, cargo space and weight are at a premium for out-of-this-world manned missions. To become an astronaut, you need more than just good vision, fitness, and blood pressure. You have to be at least 5'2" and no more than 6'3". No NBA centers need apply.

When you wish upon a star: Hey, kids, if you are determined to stand in line and ride every ride at a Florida theme park, wear your tallest shoes and cross your fingers. According to OrlandoFlorida.net, a tourism website, here are minimum heights for a few popular attractions:

Magic Kingdom	
Goofy's Barnstormer	35"
Stitch's Great Escape	40"
Big Thunder Mountain	40"
Splash Mountain	40"
Space Mountain	44"

Epcot	
Test Track	40"
Soarin'	40"

MGM Studios	
Star Tours	40"
Mission Space	44"

Off you go into the wild blue yonder—if you're just right in height: To apply as an F-22 fighter pilot for the U.S. Air Force, your sitting height must be between 34 and 40 inches; standing height from 5'4" to 6'5". But before you measure, keep in mind that you also can't have allergies or any history of asthma or hay fever after age 12. Oh, and you have to be smart, physically fit, and okay with a training regimen that would make most people pass out, throw up, or both. What are you waiting for?

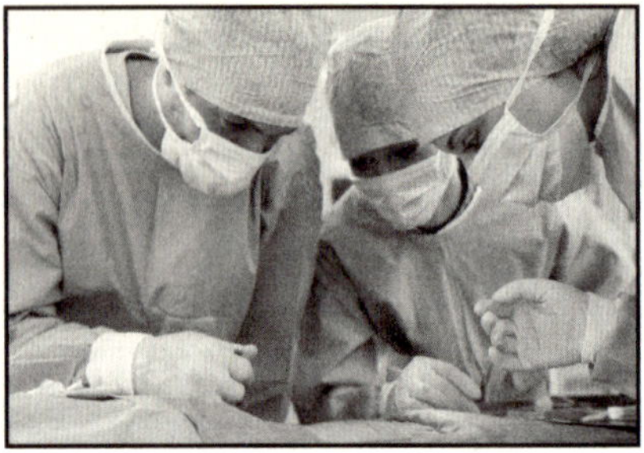

American Diseases

When it comes to general health, there has never been a better time to be alive in America. But people still get sick and die—especially from heart conditions—and one thing the country is pretty good at is adding up the numbers. Here are a few.

According to the American Heart Association (AHA), more than 81 million people in the country have at least one cardiovascular disease (CVD). Look around you. That's an average of one in every three people you see. Find a clock with a second hand and watch it for 38 seconds: That's how often an American dies from some form of heart disease.

It's tempting to wonder if this is a new health crisis—something driven by, say, too much TV watching and too many french fries. But the National Center for Health Statistics notes that, in every year but one since 1900, CVD has been the leading cause of death in the United States. The only exception was 1918, when a flu pandemic killed millions worldwide, including more than 650,000 in the U.S.

Nearly half of people with cardiovascular disease are 60 or older, according to the AHA.

Cardiovascular Disease Cases in the U.S.

Condition	Cases
High blood pressure	74.5 million
Coronary heart disease	17.6 million
Heart failure	5.8 million
Stroke	6.4 million
Congenital defects	650,000 to 1.3 million

Source: American Heart Association

Certain heart diseases affect some American racial groups more than others. For example, high blood pressure, or hypertension, affects nearly one-third of African Americans, compared to rates in the low-20% range for most other groups.

Cardiovascular Disease Rates

Group	Heart Disease	Hypertension	Stroke
White	12.1%	23.3%	2.7%
African American	10.2%	31.8%	3.6%
Hispanic	8.1%	21.0%	2.6%
Asian	5.2%	21.0%	1.8%

Source: 2008 Vital Health Stat 10, NCHS/NHIS

Alzheimer's Disease

Approximately 5.3 million people in the nation have Alzheimer's disease. The vast majority of those are 65 or older, but an estimated 200,000 people under 65 have younger-onset Alzheimer's, according to the National Alzheimer's Association.

The disease is the seventh-leading cause of death in the country, and the trend is upward, unlike several other leading causes of death. The association estimates annual costs of the disease and other dementia conditions to be nearly $175 billion. In part because they live longer than men, women are more likely to suffer from the disease.

Alzheimer's: Key Facts About the "Long Goodbye"

- Alzheimer's is the reason for 70% of dementia in Americans over the age of 70.
- From 2010 to 2030, the number of Americans with the disease is projected to rise by 50% to nearly 8 million, as the entire baby boom generation turns 65 or older.

Diabetes

Diabetes affects more than 23 million men, women, and children in America, and it costs society nearly $175 billion annually, according to the American Diabetes Association. Experts say that nearly 6 million Americans haven't been diagnosed and another 57 million citizens have pre-diabetes—their blood glucose is above normal.

The disease can lead to an array of serious conditions. For example, it's the top cause of new blindness cases and kidney failure for adults between 20 and 74.

Cancer

According to the Centers for Disease Control and Prevention, more than 700,000 American men learned they had a form of cancer, and more than 290,000 died from cancer, in 2006. Prostate cancer was the leading type by far, with more than 200,000 diagnosed cases, followed by lung/bronchus and colon/rectal.

The CDC says that breast cancer, lung cancer, and colorectal cancer are the most prevalent cancers among U.S. women. Lung cancer actually is the leading cause of cancer deaths for women.

But the trends for most cancers among women and men are encouraging. According to *Cancer Statistics 2010,* cancer rates declined 1.3% every year from 2000 through 2006 among men, and half a percent among women from 1998 to 2006. Cancer death rates were down over the past decade, too.

Sadly, cancer is the second-leading cause of deaths of children under 15. But improvements in detection and treatment have improved a child's five-year cancer survival odds to nearly four in five.

Arthritis

Almost 50 million American adults have a form of arthritis, and that number is expected to grow by more than half as the population continues to age. According to the latest National Health Interview Survey, the most common form is osteoarthritis, which affects 27 million people. Rheumatoid arthritis, a potentially crippling form of the disease, hits approximately 1.3 million Americans. Another form of arthritis, gout, affects 3 million people, most of them men.

Rare Diseases

Not all diseases are as common as heart disease and cancer. An astonishing 7,000 conditions are classified as rare diseases by the National Institutes of Health Office of Rare Diseases. Each affects fewer than 200,000 people. These illnesses, which affect nearly 30 million Americans overall, are often caused by genetic conditions. Examples include fibrodysplasia ossificans progressive, a rare, immobilizing disease that affects approximately 2,500 people worldwide.

Better known examples include the hereditary bleeding condition hemophilia, which affects 20,000 Americans, and sickle cell disease, which affects approximately 50,000 people in the country, most of them African Americans.

But among these conditions, few are as rare as Anderson-Tawil syndrome, a condition that causes periodic paralysis. Approximately 100 people in the world have been diagnosed with the syndrome.

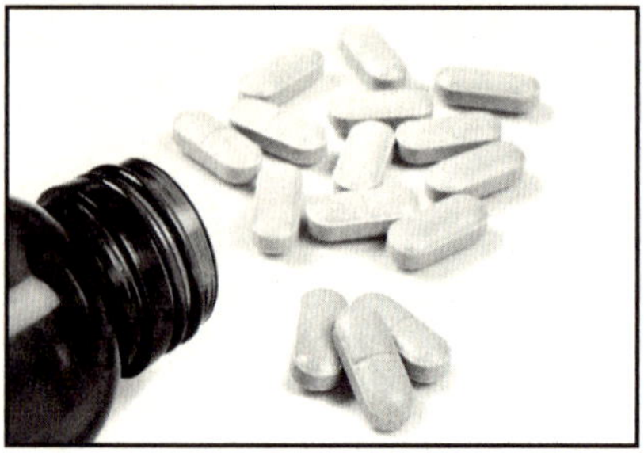

Health Remedies

Americans spend so much time and money curing or preventing medical conditions that it sometimes seems that health care, not baseball, is the great American pastime.

According to the Centers for Disease Control and Prevention (CDC), Americans make more than a billion visits a year to doctors' offices, health clinics, and emergency rooms. Nearly half of Americans will take at least one prescription drug this month, and one in 10 citizens will take five or more! It's part of a sprawling U.S. health care economy that totals $2 trillion a year.

Most Commonly Used Prescription Drugs in the U.S. by Age Group

6 and under	Penicillin antibiotics
7 to 11	Bronchodilators (asthma treatment)
12 to 19	Central nervous system stimulants
20 to 59	Antidepressants
60 and older	Cholesterol-lowering drugs

Source: National Center for Health Statistics

Not all of the cures people seek are from conventional methods, according to the National Center for Complementary and Alternative Medicine. Approximately 38% of adults use some form of complementary and alternative medicine, or CAM.

The National Health Interview Survey revealed that Americans spend $34 billion a year on CAM products. That's about one-third as much as they spend on conventional drugs. The most frequently used CAM therapies are natural products, meditation and relaxation techniques, chiropractic and osteopathic treatment, massage, yoga, and acupuncture. Americans seek out those treatments for everything from back pain to colds, depression, intestinal ailments, and high cholesterol.

Top Natural Health Products Used by Adults

1. Fish oil/Omega 3
2. Glucosamine
3. Echinacea
4. Flaxseed oil
5. Ginseng
6. Combination herb pills
7. Ginkgo biloba

Some treatments are more controversial. Homeopathic drugs, highly diluted forms of conventional drugs, and, in some cases, substances such as sulphur or arsenic have made a comeback in the past 20 years in the United States. Despite controversy over whether homeopathic medicine is no more effective than a placebo, the CDC estimates than 4% of Americans use homeopathy anyway.

Another controversial area of "treatment" draws regular attention from federal authorities: clinics outside the U.S. patronized by desperate American cancer victims. These facilities may use treatments such as magnetic fields, hydrogen peroxide, or other dubious methods.

What We Eat

Put down your knife and fork for a minute and read about what Americans are eating. From meat to dairy products to cereals and nuts, the 300-plus million of us are really good at what Beldar, the fictional Conehead alien of TV and film, called "consuming mass quantities."

Over the last three decades of the 20th century, daily consumption of calories by Americans rose by 22% for women, to about 1,875 calories, according to sources including the Centers for Disease Control and Prevention. For men, the increase was smaller, only 7%, but they had a big head start: Average daily consumption for men is more than 2,600 calories.

The U.S. Department of Agriculture's Economic Research Service estimates that each year the average American consumes about 62 pounds of beef, 47 pounds of pork, and 60 pounds of chicken. That's a lot of burgers and wings.

If you're stopping by the store on the way home from work, it's a good thing you're not buying eggs and milk for the whole neighborhood: The USDA estimates that each person downs four or five eggs and between a quart and a half gallon of milk a week. What else is on our plates? Here are the per-person averages for other selected food items:

Food	**Annual Consumption**
Flour and cereal	196.9 pounds
Caloric sweeteners	136.3 pounds
Yogurt	21 half pints
Fish and shellfish	16.3 pounds
Ice cream	14.0 pounds
American cheese	12.8 pounds
Mozzarella cheese	10.9 pounds
Cream cheese	2.6 pounds
Butter	4.7 pounds
Margarine	4.5 pounds
Coffee (beans)	9.6 pounds
Peanuts	6.3 pounds

Source: USDA; Census Bureau's The 2010 Statistical Abstract

Before you get the idea that all Americans eat is pork chops, pizza, and cereal that's "shot with sugar, through and through," here's some other news: Apparently, mothers are actually succeeding in getting their children to eat their fruits and vegetables, since the average American consumes hundreds of pounds of them each year.

Fruit or Vegetable	**Annual Consumption**
All fruits	263 pounds
Bananas	26.0 pounds
Apples	16.4 pounds
Watermelons	16.3 pounds
Grapes	8.0 pounds
Oranges (fresh)	7.5 pounds

Pineapples	5.0 pounds
Fresh vegetables	202.2 pounds
Potatoes	39.2 pounds
Onions	21.7 pounds
Lettuce	20.3 pounds
Tomatoes	20.3 pounds
Corn	9.1 pounds
Carrots	9.0 pounds
Broccoli	6.0 pounds
Processed vegetables	214.7 pounds
Potatoes for chips	18.7 pounds

Source: USDA; Census Bureau's The 2010 Statistical Abstract

Apparently not everyone hates broccoli, although that dislike got plenty of attention when President George H. W. Bush said, "[I] haven't liked it since I was a little kid and my mother made me eat it. I'm president of the United States, and I'm not going to eat any more broccoli."

Researchers continue to explore the genetic and cultural reasons why some tastes offend certain people but not others. Some people find the taste of cilantro repulsive, for example, and can detect its presence in minute levels in a cooked meal. Other people like the salsa-enhancing herb so much that they might consider *Cilantro* as a middle name for their next child.

An unscientific but entertaining online poll by AOL and Slashfood in 2007 found that the top 10 most hated foods (broccoli didn't make the list) were, in order, liver, lima beans, mayonnaise, mushrooms, eggs, okra, beets, Brussels sprouts, tuna, and gelatin.

Coffee, Tea, and Then Some

To wash down those mass quantities, Americans turn to a variety of beverages. Most but not all of them are nonalcoholic, including an incredible 48 gallons of soft drinks per American every year! Other

USDA statistics show a slow decline from 1980 through 2007 in milk and beer consumed.

Beverage	Annual Consumption
Soft drinks	48.8 gallons
Bottled water	29.1 gallons
Beer	25.7 gallons
Coffee	24.6 gallons
Wine	21.8 gallons
Milk	20.7 gallons
Tea	8.4 gallons
Fruit juices	8.2 gallons
Spirits	1.4 gallons

Source: USDA; Census Bureau's The 2010 Statistical Abstract

Those numbers are per capita, but studies have shown that between one-quarter and one-third of Americans don't drink alcohol at all.

One unsettling statistic from *What We Eat in America,* a USDA study at the start of the 21st century, is that a few people drink carbonated soft drinks for breakfast. Five percent of those surveyed admitted they chase their waffles or omelet with a soda of some kind. But according to the study, solid percentages of Americans choose juice (19%), coffee (33%), or milk (46%) as their way to start the day.

Vegetarians and Vegans

A 2008 study by *Vegetarian Times* found that nearly 3% of American adults—about 7 million people—follow some type of vegetarian diet. A smaller subset are vegans, meaning they completely avoid animal products. The poll, conducted by Harris Interactive, showed that women (59%) were more likely than men to be vegetarians. The preference for a vegetarian diet seems likely to rise in coming years, since only 17.4% of vegetarians are over 55.

Sleepy America

Yawn! Across the board, in every age group, Americans are sleeping less than their grandparents did. After World War I, we averaged eight to nine hours of sleep until 1955. That year, for the first time, the average nightly amount of sleep slipped to 7.9 hours. Since then, the nation has steadily lost a few more minutes of sleep time each decade. At least in the age of 24-hour cable television, there's something to watch when you're not sleeping—or maybe that's the problem.

Either way, here are the eye-rubbing facts and trends.

Average Weeknight Daily Sleep, Men and Women in U.S.

1910	10 Hours
1918	9.0 Hours
1955	7.9 Hours
1978	7.5 Hours
2005	6.9 Hours
2010	6.7 Hours

According to Sleep in America, an annual poll by the National Sleep Foundation, Americans 18 years and older now sleep an average of 6.7 hours on weeknights. That's an hour less than Americans slept half a century earlier. Among more than 1,500 Americans surveyed annually by the Washington, D.C.-based, nonprofit organization, only 26% reported spending the recommended eight hours in dreamland, down from 38% in 2000.

The findings of the National Sleep Foundation mirror those of the Centers for Disease Control and Prevention. In a recent National Health and Interview Survey, the CDC estimated that the percentage of Americans sleeping less than six hours nightly has "increased significantly" over the last 20 years.

The Stupefying of America

As Americans sleep less—whether by choice or due to stress and other factors—the medical and economic costs of sleep deprivation continue to rise at an alarming rate. Some sleep researchers fear that if the trend continues, the nation will suffer from a lack of productivity coupled with a "dumbing down" of the national workforce.

Think you have a high IQ? Let's say you are very intelligent, with an IQ of 120. Assuming you don't smoke marijuana or suffer from early Alzheimer's, you'll be "smarter" than about 90% of Americans—but not if you fail to get eight hours of sleep a night, warns sleep researcher Stanley Coren. For each night that you get seven hours or less, Coren writes, you can temporarily lose the equivalent of one IQ point. If you stay up later and sleep only six hours, you could lose two IQ points a day. By the end of a sleep-deprived week, you could shave an amazing 15 points off your IQ, at least until you replenish your lost slumber.

The consequences can be even worse for someone of average or below-average intelligence, Coren believes. A person with an IQ of 100 who loses 15 points could wind up, temporarily, in the same league as a smart fish.

You Sleep with *What*?

Good night, Fido. When people finally settle down for a night's rest, many of them take the dog or cat to bed with them, according the National Sleep Foundation. This is more common among white Americans. Fourteen percent say they routinely sleep with one of their pets, while only 2% of people in other ethnic groups in the country do so.

Good night, John Boy. Twelve percent of people with children say they often end up sharing valuable sleeping time—or getting kicked in the head, maybe—with their children.

Separate beds. Among married people, one out of 10 sleeps alone. And one of out every five Americans told Sleep Foundation researchers that they have less sex or less interest in sex because they are just too sleepy.

Good morning, iPhone. A 2009 study by the online marketing research firm Synovate found that nearly half of people are so addicted to their smart phones that they take them to bed with them.

Staying Awake!

Many overworked Americans now lumber through their days in a stupor, propped up by frequent jolts of caffeine. In fact, the National Center on Sleep Research Disorders Research estimates that nearly 70 million Americans have sleep problems ranging from garden-variety insomnia to sleep apnea, narcolepsy, and restless leg syndrome. Is it any wonder that coffee is the world's second most traded fuel, right behind oil? Unfortunately, too much coffee is one of the most common causes of acid reflux disease and hypertension.

According to the Sleep Foundation, Americans use an amazing variety of ways to help them get through the day when all they really feel like doing is yawning. Here are the five most common things they try during the day:

Getting caffeinated. Forty percent of sleepy people drink one or two soft drinks a day; another 41% drink three or more!

Loading up on sugar and carbs. Four in 10 sleepy people cope by eating sugary or high-carbohydrate foods. Of course, as every fuzzy-brained worker can testify, that food-fueled alertness comes with a terrible price an hour or so later: the dreaded "crash" that can leave them even sleepier. Back to the donuts!

Popping pills. Sodas and junk food don't cut it for some sleepy people. About 5% report that they deal with it by taking over-the-counter or prescription medications.

Napping. More than half of Americans are likely to go to bed early on a weeknight or sleep in on the weekend after a particularly sleepy episode. More than a third said they nap when possible.

Getting more zzzs! Despite all the tricks people use to get through a sleepy day, most people get the idea that only the real thing will help them catch up on sleep.

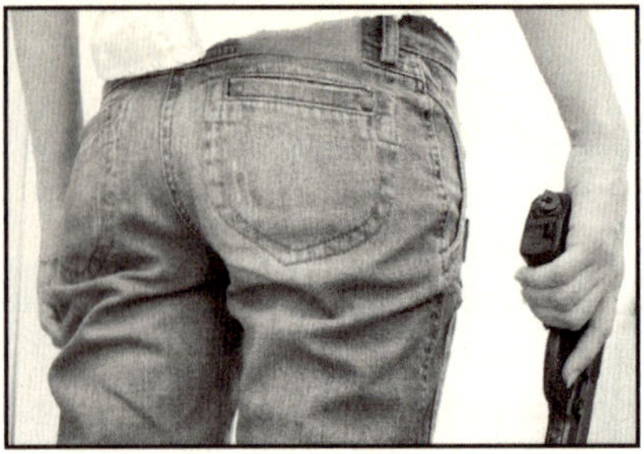

Weapons of Choice

Nearly four centuries after the first European arrivals at Jamestown hunted for dinner, Americans own and use an amazing variety of weapons. Most of them, but not all, are used for lawful purposes or are not "used" at all.

According to the National Rifle Association (NRA), which claims approximately 4 million members, there are close to 300 million privately owned firearms in the United States. Approximately 100 million of those weapons are handguns. The NRA, which advocates for gun owners' rights and sponsors education and training programs, also estimates that more than 40% of households in the country have at least one firearm.

Number	Firearm Fact
300 million	Number of privately owned U.S. firearms
100 million	Handguns privately owned
70+ million	American gun owners
14.5 million	Annual hunting licenses sold in the U.S.

63,000	NRA-certified gun instructors
800,000	Participate in NRA firearm courses each year

The most recent Gallup survey of gun ownership in the country confirmed the NRA's finding that more than 40% of households own a firearm. Two-thirds of those gun owners told Gallup that they owned the weapon for protection against crime. Slightly more than 40% reported that they used their guns for hunting. Men (63%) were much more likely than women (45%) to tell Gallup they used guns for hunting.

Who Owns the Guns, According to Gallup

Households	42%
Individuals	30%
Men	47%
Women	13%
Whites	33%
Nonwhites	18%
Republicans	41%
Democrats	23%

The Brady Center to Prevent Gun Violence takes the other side from the NRA in the long-lasting political debate about the benefits of gun control laws. Nevertheless, the Brady Center publishes similar facts about gun ownership in the country, gathered from an array of law enforcement and other government sources:

- Approximately 4.5 million new firearms, 2 million of them handguns, will be sold this year in the country, according to the U.S. Bureau of Alcohol, Tobacco, and Firearms (ATF).
- The ATF says that people will also buy another 2 million secondhand guns.

- The Police Foundation estimates that gun owners discard approximately 36,000 guns every year.

The Brady position is that gun violence is more frequent in places where there are more guns, and where gun laws are few or not enforced.

Whatever you believe about the merits of gun control, just how many firearms may be present in your neighborhood depends a great deal on where you live in America. According to the Centers for Disease Control and Prevention (CDC), in states on the high end of the gun-ownership chart (such as Wyoming), nearly two-thirds of households own at least one gun. In Hawaii, guns can be found in less than 10% of homes.

A CDC ranking of deaths attributed to firearms shows striking regional variations, too. All of the top five states in the rankings are in the Gulf Coast or Far West regions, while four of the bottom five states are clustered in New England.

States with the Highest and Lowest Rates of Death by Firearms

1. Louisiana
2. Alabama
3. Alaska and Mississippi (tie)
5. Nevada

...

46. New York
47. Connecticut
48. Rhode Island
49. Massachusetts
50. Hawaii

Sources: Centers for Disease Control and Prevention; National Center for Injury Control and Prevention

Recent FBI statistics on the types of weapons used in murders make it pretty clear that a gun is most often the murder weapon. Among the more than 13,000 U.S. murders in 2009 for which the bureau received detailed case information, more than 9,100 were committed with some type of firearm. Knives and other sharp instruments accounted for more than one in every 10 murders. And slightly more than 800 murders were committed by people using their hands, fists, or feet.

FBI Breakdown of Murder in the U.S. by Type of Weapon

Weapon	Murders
Handguns	6,452
Rifles	348
Shotguns	418
Other firearms	1,928
Knives, etc.	1,825
Other weapons	1,864
Hands, etc.	801
All weapons	13,636

When it comes to robberies involving a weapon, guns are once again the most likely weapon, according to the FBI crime report. Of more than 350,000 such crimes studied—only a fraction of the overall robberies in the country—almost exactly half were committed with a firearm. Only one of every 13 robberies involved a knife or other cutting instrument. But a surprising 144,000 were what the FBI calls "strong-arm" robberies. Apparently, hands and feet are a major weapon of choice for perpetrators of property crime.

Firearms are indeed a big business in the U.S., according to the ATF's 2010 report on firearms manufacture and export. Nearly 1.9 million pistols and revolvers were manufactured in the U.S. in 2009. Included were more than 600,000 of the .38-caliber pistol favored as standard issue by many police departments.

In addition, ATF statistics show that more than 2.1 million rifles, more than 750,000 shotguns, and approximately 133,000 other firearms were manufactured during the year. Since less than one-quarter of all firearms built in the U.S. are exported, the vast majority are available for sale to owners ranging from private citizens to police and military agencies.

Are Bare Hands Really Weapons?

It is a myth that people with advanced training in martial arts have to register their hands or bodies with the local police as "lethal weapons." However, there's no doubt that a significant number of Americans would like to know how to defend themselves with their hands instead of with a gun.

The U.S. Martial Arts Federation certifies more than 500 black belts, but a much larger number—more than 4 million Americans—participate on some level in martial arts programs around the country every year, according to the National Sporting Goods Association. The vast majority of those participants get involved for the physical and mental benefits of the training, experts say, not because they want to make themselves into weapons.

Although the popularity of karate, tai chi, and other martial arts programs may have peaked during the aftermath of the blockbuster hit movie *Karate Kid* and its less critically admired sequels, Hollywood has sensed that "kid overcomes challenges through martial arts" is a theme with lasting potential. A 2010 remake of *Karate Kid* had already grossed more than $175 million at the box office by late 2010. Wax on, wax off!

Tasers, Bows, and Arrows

Tasers, on the other hand, really are a growth business in the American weapons industry. Demand for the "electronic control device," which was named as a tribute to Thomas A. Swift's Electric Rifle from a children's book series, continues to boom. Tasers are used by more than 12,000 law enforcement agencies, according to a CBS News report.

Police often favor the device for subduing unruly subjects because of the lower risk of lethal consequences compared to conventional weapons. Not everyone agrees. Amnesty International claims that in the past decade, more than 350 Americans died after being shocked by police Tasers. The group contends that number could grow because police now see Tasers as a "tool of routine force" and not just an alternative to guns.

More than 43,000 police officers are trained to operate Tasers. But the real growth for the devices, according to the Taser company, is among private citizens: More than 190,000 people already own a consumer version of the weapon. Not everyone is enthusiastic about that trend. Taser.com says that private sales of the devices are prohibited by law in New York, New Jersey, Rhode Island, Michigan, Wisconsin, Massachusetts, and Hawaii. A few cities, including Omaha and Washington, have laws against private Taser ownership. And New Jersey even bans the use of Tasers by law enforcement. Forget about it!

So unless you live in one of those places, the next time you open your neighbor's front door without knocking, you may want to at least know the phrase "Don't Tase me, bro!" That line became a nationwide sensation in 2007 after a viral Internet video showed a University of Florida student being zapped by police with a Taser device after an altercation during a political forum that featured U.S. Senator John Kerry.

They aren't nearly as high-tech as Tasers, but bows and arrows are still the weapon of choice for a surprising number of Americans who participate in hunting. According to data published by the Michigan Department of Natural Resources, more than one-third of the nation's 14 million licensed American hunters have hunted with a bow at least once in the past two years. Nearly all of them—94% of bow hunters—were hunting whitetail or other deer species.

Leading Causes of Death in America

Some people worry constantly about which scary thing will be the cause of their death some day. It probably doesn't help that movies, novels, and real newscasts—now played 24 hours a day—are filled with lurid tales of fatal occurrences.

Will it be a plane crash, a mugger, a poisonous snake, a fire, or some other frightening thing that ends your life? Maybe, but according to the National Center for Health Statistics and the U.S. Department of Health and Human Services, there are other things much more likely to kill you. Diseases and other health ailments, they say, make up 12 of the top 15 causes of death in the United States.

In 2007, the year of the Center's most recent full accounting of the Grim Reaper's work, slightly more than 2.4 million people died in the United States. That works out to just under 800 deaths for every 100,000 people. So your odds of living are much better than your odds of dying. And life expectancy continues to improve: The average American lives to be nearly 80—but women live an average of five years longer than men.

No matter who you are, death catches up with everyone sooner or later. When it does, it will probably be from one of these 15 causes:

Cause of Death in America

1. Heart disease
2. Cancer
3. Stroke
4. Lower respiratory disease
5. Accidents
6. Alzheimer's disease
7. Diabetes
8. Influenza and pneumonia
9. Kidney disease
10. Septicemia
11. Suicide
12. Liver disease
13. Hypertension
14. Parkinson's disease
15. Homicide

Those familiar killers account for more than 80% of deaths in the country, year in and year out. Stroke has trended mostly lower since 1958, but there's still a one in 28 chance it will get you.

Fewer smokers and better treatment options have improved the odds of avoiding or surviving cancer, but there's still a one in seven chance that it will be the cause of an American's death. People take better care of their hearts these days, but heart disease, still at the top of the list, is the cause of one of every six deaths.

What Are the Chances?

The National Safety Council's 2010 list of the 50 most likely causes of death in the nation includes several surprising threats that are far below the familiar health causes, but high enough on the list to get your attention. You could die as a result of:

- A deadly encounter with a reptile (50th most likely). But don't worry too much, since there's just a one in 3.8 million chance.
- Riding in a streetcar (49th)
- Being blown up by fireworks (45th)
- War (38th). For Americans, this usually applies only to the brave people who join the armed services. Nevertheless, war still causes one of every 137,000 deaths.
- Legal execution (33rd)
- Choking on food (19th). Learn the Heimlich maneuver so you or a friend won't be one of the one in 4,400 deaths resulting from accidentally breathing food instead of swallowing it.

Where you live has a lot to do with your chances of dying, too. In the 2007 HHS statistics, West Virginia had the highest age-adjusted death rate, 951 per 100,000 residents. Hawaii was more than just a nice place to get a tan: The Aloha State's death rate was 607 per 100,000 people, more than 20% lower than the national average.

Not as Common, But No Fun Either

Farther down the list—sometimes way down the list—are these other causes of death in America:

HIV. One welcome absence from the list of top 15 killers is human immunodeficiency virus, or HIV, which was last on that list in 1997. Since then, the HIV death rate has declined each year, although the condition still caused more than 11,000 deaths in 2007.

Taser guns. Amnesty International reported recently that there were 351 Taser-related deaths in the United States between mid-2001 and mid-2008. Stun gun manufacturers and many law enforcement officials respond that safe, appropriate use of Tasers probably prevents many other deaths.

Your cell phone. One National Safety Council study estimates that cell phone use contributes to 6% of all vehicle crashes, resulting in 2,600 deaths per year. Although it's not as likely to kill you as a heart attack, is texting your sister while driving really worth it?

Work Can Kill

More than half of injury-related deaths happen at home or in public settings outside the workplace, according to the National Safety Council. Only 8% are work-related. But some jobs are more dangerous than others. You may be surprised to find that the Bureau of Labor Statistics ranks America's top 10 most dangerous occupations this way:

Dangerous Jobs

1. Fishing industry jobs
2. Logging
3. Pilots and flight engineers
4. Farmers and ranchers
5. Roofers
6. Iron and steel workers
7. Trash and recycling collectors
8. Industrial machine workers
9. Truckers, sales/delivery drivers
10. Construction workers

Fishing was more than three times as likely to kill workers than the second-place profession, logging. And although a few specialty fishermen can make big money, the median annual income for fishermen is less than $25,000. Not the ideal ratio of risk to reward.

Misbehavin'

States of Crime and Punishment

6ft
6
5ft
5
4ft
4
3ft
3

Crime and Punishment

In the age of 24/7 cable television news, just turning on the TV could give anyone the impression that crime is rampant in America. Nearly any day you may see live or recorded coverage of a bank hostage crisis, a high-speed chase of a criminal by police on the freeway, or the latest developments in a missing-child or high-profile murder case. Fictional television only serves to enhance the sense of a crime-ridden society. Popular TV crime dramas include *Criminal Minds*, *Bones*, *Law & Order*, and a revival of the *Hawaii Five-O* series.

But according to federal crime logs, the rate of violent crime in the country is at its lowest level since 1973, the first year of the annual Criminal Victimization report by the Bureau of Justice Statistics. During the first decade of the 21st century, property crimes fell 29% and violent crimes dropped by 39%.

Crime may be down, but that's not to say there's nothing to worry about.

Who Murders Whom

Of the 7,650 murders in 2009 for which the FBI recorded the relationship between victim and murderer, an American murder victim was most likely to be killed by an acquaintance (38%) or a total stranger (22%).

Killer's Relationship to Victim

1. Acquaintance
2. Stranger
3. Husband
4. Boyfriend
5. Friend
6. Other relative
7. Parent
8. Wife
9. Girlfriend
10. Neighbor
11. Child
12. Sibling
13. Employee

Source: FBI

FBI statistics show that more than 1.3 million violent crimes happened in 2009. The trend has been lower nearly every year in the past decade. But that still equates to more than 425 violent crimes per 100,000 people in the U.S. The vast majority of those were aggravated assaults (61%), followed by robbery (31%), forcible rape (6.7%), and murder, which accounted for just over 1% of all violent crimes in the year.

It's no big surprise that guns play a big role in violent offenses. Some type of firearm was used in two-thirds of the nation's murders, in 42% of all robberies, and in one of every five aggravated assaults.

Modern Bank Robbers

It would be easy to think of bank robbery as something more common in the era of Al Capone and other gangsters, but the FBI is still busy investigating bank robberies in the 21st century. During just the second quarter of 2010, there were more than 1,100 bank robbery crimes in the U.S. Although that was down from the same quarter in the previous year, the FBI said that robbers took more than $8.4 million, of which only slightly more than $1 million was recovered.

The Habits of Bank Robbers

- Fridays are the most common day for bank crimes.
- Most bank jobs happen between 9 A.M. and 11 A.M.
- Ninety-five percent of bank robberies don't involve violence, and most involve written or verbal demands, not guns.
- The biggest region for bank robberies is the West.

Who's Getting Arrested, and for What

In the most recent year summarized by FBI statistics, law enforcement officers made more than 13.6 million arrests. That doesn't include arrests for traffic violations.

Arrests by Gender and Race

74.7%	Males
24.3%	Females
69.1%	Whites
28.3%	Blacks
2.6%	Other races

Source: FBI

Of the more than 13 million arrests per year, the top four types were:

Property crimes	1.7 million
Drug violations	1.6 million
Driving (DUI)	1.4 million
Larceny	1.3 million

For nearly every category of crime covered by the FBI's Uniform Crime Reporting program—gambling arrests are the only exception—people under 25 have the highest rates of criminal activity.

Jail, Prison, Probation, or Parole

Approximately one in every 31 American adults is on probation, on parole, or serving time in jail or prison, according to the most recent Bureau of Justice Statistics report. That's more than 7 million people, or just over 3% of the U.S. adult population.

More than two-thirds of those people aren't actually locked up. They are on parole or probation, and they are supervised in the community by local, state, or federal correctional agencies. The vast majority of people being held in jails or prisons are in state facilities. Only about 13% of all prisoners are in federal custody.

Cyber Crime Is on the Rise

One area of crime in America that is clearly a growth business is Internet and computer crime. The FBI's Internet Crime Complaint Center's annual report of incoming complaints is just the tip of the Internet iceberg, since it doesn't cover all online crime activity reported to other law enforcement.

Top Five Categories of Cyber Crimes Reported to Law Enforcement in 2009

1. Non-delivered merchandise or payments
2. Identity theft
3. Credit card fraud
4. Auction fraud
5. Computer fraud (damage, vandalism, etc.)

Source: FBI Internet Crime Complaint Center

The more than 330,000 complaints received in 2009 included financial losses of nearly $560 million.

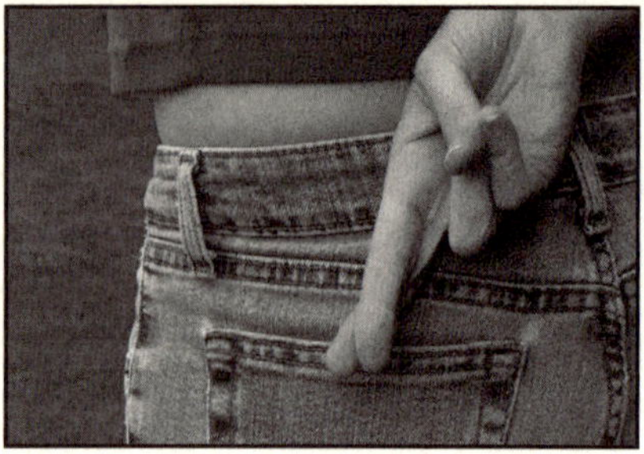

Cheating to Get Ahead

Cheating scandals in the adult world have become so common that they have their own TV shows, such as CNBC's *American Greed: Scams, Scoundrels and Scandals.* From governors to golfing legends, CEOs to ministers, an episode—or habit—of cheating can instantly short-circuit a successful career in the world of 24/7 news coverage.

But it's not just famous people who cheat. According to the Culture and Media Institute's National Cultural Values Survey, a third of Americans admit they would cheat by working an under-the-table job while collecting government unemployment. And one in four say they would keep quiet and pocket the money if a restaurant failed to bill them for an item. Studies have shown that between one and three of every 10 married Americans have cheated with another sexual partner.

The nonprofit Josephson Institute of Ethics has surveyed thousands of Americans and found that:

- Youth matters: 51% of children 17 and younger think lying and cheating is essential for success, compared to 10% of adults over 50.

- Seven percent of young adults admit to having inflated an insurance claim, compared to 2% of people over 50.
- People who cheated in high school are three times as likely to lie to a customer, twice as likely to lie to their bosses, and slightly more likely to cheat on their taxes.

Long before they face those choices, many young Americans have cheated, usually in school. A Josephon survey of high school athletes found that nearly two-thirds have cheated in school, slightly higher than non-athletes.

A Duke University study found either more cheaters or more people willing to be honest about their cheating: Three-quarters of high school students admitted to cheating on tests, and a stunning 90% had copied another student's paper.

Digital Cheating Rises

A Common Sense Media survey of teenagers and their parents found that cell phones and the Internet are the new frontiers of cheating.

Teens	Cheating
65%	Say others in school cheat with cell phones
52%	Have used the Internet to cheat in school
38%	Have committed Internet-based plagiarism
41%	Think using cell-phone notes on a test is serious cheating
19%	Think it's cheating to claim a downloaded paper as their own
35%	Of those with cell phones have used their phone to cheat

Use and Abuse of Drugs

In the science fiction film *The Matrix*, hero figure Neo is given a choice of taking one of two pills. Taking a blue pill will return him to a simulated existence, where he would be unaware of a horrifying reality controlled by machines. The red pill will help him learn the truth and fight for human freedom.

In today's reality, there are far more than two pills available, and Americans take an extraordinarily large number of them every day to both good and bad effect.

The latest National Survey on Drug Use and Health (2009) found that nearly 22 million Americans 12 and older were using illegal drugs. Those drugs included marijuana; various forms of cocaine, heroin, hallucinogens, and inhalants; and some prescription drugs used illegally.

Where the Drugs Are

Region	Rate of Illegal Use by Americans, 12+
West	10.3%
Northeast	9.2%

Midwest	7.9%
South	7.8%

More than 16 million Americans 12 and older were using marijuana, making it by far the most common illegal drug choice. Nonmedically used psychotherapeutic prescription drugs were next with 7 million users. Other illegal uses included:

- Cocaine, 1.6 million users
- Hallucinogens including Ecstasy, 1.3 million users
- Methamphetamine, 731,000 users

Nonmedical use of painkillers may conjure up images of shady characters selling pills in an alley, but the truth may be scarier: More than 55% who abused pain medications got them from a friend or relative. Another 17% acquired meds from a doctor. Less than 5% bought drugs from a drug dealer or other person unknown to them. And despite those pesky spam e-mails everyone gets for cheap pharmaceuticals, less than half of 1 percent of people misused painkillers that they bought online.

People in their 50s are showing a slight decline in drug abuse. But researchers think that's just because Baby Boomers, who have higher drug use tendencies, are growing out of that group. The 60-plus Americans are about to become the trendsetters, and not just for prescriptions for cholesterol or erectile dysfunction.

Prescription Drugs: A Booming Business

Not all substances are abused, of course. Innovation in pharmaceutical research since the mid-20th century has improved many lives. But the rate of pill popping, even the legal kind, is growing. A recent federal National Health and Nutrition Examination Survey found that 88% of Americans over 60 take at least one prescription drug, and there's an even chance it's a cholesterol-lowering substance. More than a third of seniors take at least five prescription medications a month!

Children are more likely to be taking antibiotics (particularly young children) or drugs for attention deficit hyperactivity disorder.

All those pills add up to a huge U.S. industry. Americans spend more than $230 billion on prescription drugs, more than twice the outlay from a decade ago.

Booze and Tobacco

Not all substance abuse comes in pill form. The 2009 National Survey on Drug Use and Health found that more than 130 million people in the nation drink alcoholic beverages. For most, that means a couple of beers or cocktails now and then. But nearly one-fourth of Americans 12 and older participate in binge drinking, which is five or more drinks per occasion at least once a month. Seventeen million people are heavy drinkers—five or more binges a month.

Underage Drinking, Americans 12 to 20

Racial Group	Alcohol Use
Whites	30.4%
Hispanics	25.1%
American Indians or Alaska Natives	22%
African Americans	20.4%
Asians	16.1%

Where Kids 12 to 20 Drink	
Someone else's home	55.9%
Their own home	29.2%

Although one-third of young people either bought their most recent drink themselves or gave money to someone else who made the purchase, the drinks are too often provided by someone else at no charge.

Who Buys Drinks for Kids

Provided for free by an unrelated adult	37.1%
Parent, guardian, other adult relative	20.6%
Another underage person	19.9%

Lighting Up

Despite significant changes in tobacco marketing and regulation in the past several decades, nearly 70 million Americans 12 and older use some form of tobacco regularly. Those using smokeless tobacco for the first time during a year jumped from 951,000 in 2002 to 1.5 million in 2009.

Tobacco Use Among Americans by Product

Cigarettes	58.7 million
Cigars	13.3 million
Smokeless tobacco	8.6 million
Pipes	2.1 million

Where People Get Started Using Drugs

Every year, more than 3 million Americans 12 and older—that's 8,500 people every day—start using an illicit drug. In nearly two-thirds of the cases, the drug of choice is marijuana. Another 29% begin with psychotherapeutic drugs including pain relievers, tranquilizers, stimulants, and sedatives. Nearly 10% start with inhalants. Only 2.1% go straight to hallucinogenic drugs.

To try and prevent illegal drug use by children, government and private advocacy groups continue to stress prevention messages. More than 75% of youths see or hear anti-drug or anti-alcohol abuse messages each year. But parental influence is still the key: Only 5% of Americans 12 to 17 whose parents strongly disapprove of marijuana use report trying it anyway, compared to 31% experimentation by those who don't think of their parents as strongly disapproving.

The Truth About Lying

According to legend, a young George Washington confessed that he killed a cherry tree with a hatchet. "I cannot tell a lie," the future president supposedly told his father. In fact, Washington's biographer made the whole thing up just to make a point about his subject's honesty.

Today, Americans often tell the truth, but they are also capable of stretching it pretty far. How far? How frequently do they lie? It depends on whom you ask, and whether you believe them.

Psychologists report that a small, unknown number of Americans suffer from mythomania, or compulsive lying, an often misdiagnosed mental illness. There is no such excuse for the rest of us, although many people are willing to provide one.

An Associated Press–Ipsos poll found that most Americans think lying is okay some of the time, especially if you lie to avoid hurting another person's feelings. But lest you think all lying is based on admirable motivations, consider these findings:

Liar, Liar, Pants on Fire

52% Say lying is never justified (but are they telling the truth?)
40% Say it's fair to embellish the truth for a more interesting story
40% Think it's okay to lie to children about a parent's bad behavior
33% Are okay with lying about their age or staying home from work
39% Say they have never lied or cheated (but 10% of those who "never lie" admitted on the next question to lying within the past week!)

When Americans stretch the truth, social pressure may play a role. Sociologists working for the United Church of Christ compared actual church attendance against what Americans reported in public opinion surveys. They found that 40% of Protestants say they go to church services, but only 20% actually attend. Half of Roman Catholics tell pollsters they go to Mass, but only 28% actually do.

Media reports have featured claims that the average American lies once or twice a day. But Michigan State University researchers who reviewed a large body of data on lying believe that most of the prevarication is done by a few prolific liars.

And there's more good news. A 2009 study by the Girl Scout Research Institute found that young people are less likely to lie now than 20 years ago. The scenario: A friend brags about destroying school property, and the principal asks you what happened. According to the institute's report, this is how the kids responded:

	Today	**20 Years Ago**
Would tell the truth	33%	24%
Would deny it	27%	36%

There's hope for us yet!

What's on Our Minds

Americans' Beliefs and Opinions

Our Paranormal Beliefs

Americans don't hesitate to let pollsters know what they believe about government policies, about conspiracy theories of the Kennedy assassination, or even what they like to eat for breakfast. So it's not surprising that they'll also go on the record about their beliefs in poltergeists, extraterrestrials, and vampires.

According to a wide range of surveys over the past decade, a significant number of Americans believe that the Earth has been visited by aliens and that the government is covering up the truth.

Life magazine and Roper polls at the start of the 21st century both found that roughly half of the population believes that UFOs are real. Several surveys since then have shown that, if anything, the belief is growing.

A recent AOL poll of more than 130,000 Internet users found that 93% believe there is life elsewhere in the universe, and eight of 10 people believe our planet has been visited by some of those aliens. A similar survey by MSNBC found that nearly two-thirds of Americans agree on the likelihood of alien visitation. And one more reason to smile and agree with the sentiment of the Randy Newman song "I Love L.A." is this finding from a 2009 poll by the *Los Angeles Times*: More than 71% of readers thought their hometown should establish an Extraterrestrial Affairs Commission.

Paranormal Is Just Normal to Many

Analysts at the Gallup organization have found that Americans are relatively open to belief in several paranormal phenomena:

37% That houses can be haunted
25% Astrology can affect people's lives
24% Extraterrestrials have visited Earth
21% The living can communicate with the dead
21% Witches exist
Source: Gallup

Men and women differ somewhat in their willingness to believe, according to Gallup. A solid 42% of American women think houses can be haunted, compared to 31% of men. Slightly more than half of American men think real extraterrestrials have visited Earth, compared to 40% of women.

A Fox News poll got similar results: One in four people said they believe in witches, and about one-third think ghosts are real. Even a few celebrities have been willing to tell their personal stories of ghostly encounters as part of the *Celebrity Ghost Stories* series on the cable TV network Biography Channel. Here are a few selected celebrities and their ghost stories, according to Biography.com:

Celebrity	Ghost Experience
Joan Collins	A vengeful ghost at a dinner party
Shirley Jones	A ghost who played with fire
Lindsay Wagner	A teenage ghost

Joan Rivers	A voodoo priestess and an angry ghost
David Carradine	Encounter with wife's late, former husband

ESP

Most people—certainly many children—have played a game to test their extrasensory perception (ESP): "What number am I thinking of?" or "Guess which card is next in the deck." But beyond the fun and games, a fair number of people share some belief in knowledge of other minds and other paranormal mental abilities. Gallup polls over the past decade have consistently found that nearly half of Americans believe in ESP.

Most scientists are not in that number. A recent survey of members of the National Academy of Sciences found that 96% are skeptical of ESP, although 4% support parapsychology and one in 10 thinks parapsychological research is worthwhile. Parapsychologists use scientific methods to look into such things as near-death experiences, mental telepathy, and remote viewing.

Vampires

Fascination with vampire stories is nothing new in America. From the early Count Dracula movies starring Bela Lugosi and Lon Chaney, to the bestselling Anne Rice vampire novels of the 1970s and 1980s, to the current frenzy over the *Twilight* books and movies, Americans just love to be scared—or seduced—by fictional vampires. According to a Fox News poll on the topic, however, only a few people actually believe that vampires are real: 4% overall, including 6% of men and 2% of women.

Americans may not believe, but they sure do like the stories. The *Twilight* fantasy romance novels have spent more than four years on the weekly *New York Times* Best Seller list in the Children's Series Books category. And three film adaptations of the novels had by mid-2010 grossed over $1.7 billion at the box office worldwide, with two more installments bound to add to that total.

Time Travel

Americans are so obsessed these days with managing their time that it's not surprising that more than a few of them are interested in the possibility of getting in a time machine and going back to start the day over—or change history. An admittedly unscientific online poll by CNN recently found that 30% of participants actually believe time travel will be possible someday.

Unfortunately, two geniuses famous for their work on time-space science haven't given us much encouragement. Albert Einstein, whose game-changing theories revolutionized modern physics, came to believe late in his life that the past, present, and future—and space—all exist as one solid reality. In other words, there's no time to which you can travel. You're already there.

Stephen Hawking has tantalized millions with his descriptions of how humans might construct a time machine, given several enormous "ifs." But in the end, even Hawking says time travel is probably not going to happen. Those 30% of Americans will probably hold out for a third opinion.

What We're Afraid Of

During the Great Depression of the 1930s, it may have been inspirational for President Franklin D. Roosevelt to tell Americans that the only thing they had to fear was "fear itself." But since then, psychologists have catalogued a long list of more specific phobias that people suffer from in the 21st century. Some are familiar, such as arachnophobia (fear of spiders) or acrophobia (fear of heights). Others, such as fear of clowns or bicycles, are fodder for comics or for humorists on the Internet. But to anyone actually affected by a phobia, it's no laughing matter.

Anxiety Disorders

According to the National Institute of Mental Health (NIMH), approximately 15 million adults in the United States have social phobia, also known as social anxiety disorder. Their phobia may focus only on one social situation, such as speaking in public, or be so general that its victim feels anxiety anytime other people are present. These conditions usually have their origins in childhood or adolescence.

Common Social Phobias in America

Nearly 20 million Americans are affected by a specific phobia. Some 6 million struggle to cope with panic disorder, and 1.8 million are agoraphobic. American women are twice as likely as men to suffer from panic disorder. About one-third of those who suffer from panic disorder eventually become agoraphobic, a serious condition in which they feel overwhelmed by the idea of leaving home at all.

Social anxiety disorder (SAD), which is difficult to treat with medication, can wreak havoc on a person's work and home life, according to the NIMH. Compared to those with no psychiatric diagnosis, a person with SAD is less likely to have a full-time job and only a fourth as likely to have a professional job. The costs to society of SAD and other anxiety disorders include:

- more than $13 billion in annual cost of psychiatric treatments
- more than $4.1 billion in productivity losses and absenteeism for businesses

Selected Phobias from A to (Nearly) Z

Ants: Myrmecophobia
Belly buttons: Omphalophobia
Chickens: Alektorophobia
Dancing: Chorophobia
Eight (the number): Octophobia
Frogs: Batrachophobia
Garlic: Alliumphobia
Hospitals: Nosocomephobia
Injections: Trypanophobia
Justice: Dikephobia
Kissing: Philemaphobia or Philematophobia
Light: Photophobia
Mirrors: Catoptrophobia

Northern lights: Auroraphobia
Otters: Lutraphobia
Politicians: Politicophobia
Relatives: Syngenesophobia
Shadows: Sciophobia or Sciaphobia
Tests: Testophobia
Undressing in front of someone: Dishabillophobia
Ventriloquist's dummy: Automatonophobia
Water: Hydrophobia
X-rays or radiation: Radiophobia
Yellow: Xanthophobia
Source: Phobialist.com

What Are Famous Americans Afraid Of?

According to various biographies, news accounts, and even their own publicists, an all-star collection of American celebrities past and present have suffered from one or more phobias.

Some of Hollywood's most photogenic actors, including Kim Basinger and the late Marilyn Monroe, have been said to suffer from a fear of being in public. Legendary singer Barbra Streisand struggled for many years with a type of social anxiety that prevented her from performing for live audiences, despite their adulation.

NFL running back Ricky Williams nearly lost his lucrative professional football career before receiving successful treatment for a social anxiety disorder. Reporters and fans had previously misinterpreted the condition as a strange variety of shyness around strangers. John Madden, the successful NFL football coach and broadcast analyst, developed a fear of flying. He became well known for using trains—and later a custom-made motor coach—to travel around the nation to cover games.

When you consider the obstacles that some of these phobias pose, many of these famous people deserve applause for the courage it took to overcome their fears and achieve public success.

Aerophobia: Fear of Flying

John Madden	football coach, broadcaster
Aretha Franklin	Queen of Soul
Whoopi Goldberg	actor
Billy Bob Thornton	actor
Muhammad Ali	boxing champion
Ronald Reagan	president, actor

Agoraphobia: Fear of Public or Open Places

Marilyn Monroe	actress
Kim Basinger	actress

Coulrophobia: Fear of Clowns

Johnny Depp	actor

Mysophobia: Fear of Germs

Howard Hughes	billionaire entrepreneur

Hydrophobia: Fear of Water

Natalie Wood	actor (died by drowning)

Botanophobia: Fear of Plants

Christina Ricci	actor

Brontophobia: Fear of Thunder

Madonna	singer

Arachnophobia: Fear of Spiders

Andre Agassi	tennis champion

Achluophobia: Fear of the Dark

Anne Rice	vampire novelist

What We Think About the U.S. Census

By design, the official U.S. census isn't as much fun as this unofficial look at American society. And although nearly three-fourths of all households dutifully returned 2010 forms, it's worth asking: What do Americans really think of the official census?

A Rasmussen poll before the 2010 census found that:

- One of every four Americans said they weren't sure what the census does.
- Approximately 13% of Americans knew it would be illegal not to complete the census forms (it is, but enforcement is unlikely).
- Slightly more than half correctly expected the census to collect only basic information on people living in each household; another 22% expected detailed personal questions. (Detailed information collected on a longer census form distributed in the past to a random selection of households is now collected through the separate American Community Survey.)

- Men were more likely than women to think the census includes personal questions.

Pew researchers learned that one in 10 Americans believed the census would be used to locate and arrest illegal immigrants. Solid majorities—but by no means everyone—were aware that the census is used to determine the distribution of Congressional seats (64%) and determine the proper distribution of money to communities (59%).

Who Thinks the Official Census Is Important?

According to Pew, here's who believes the census is very important:

60% Americans overall
45% People under 30
71% Democrats
56% Republicans
74% African Americans
57% Whites

Census Fears

Snopes.com, which checks out Internet rumors, listed one recurring worry in 2009 and 2010 about the U.S. Census: that criminals would pose as census workers to steal information or valuables from people. News accounts during those years included several such cases, although few law enforcement sources reported that such crimes were common.

Less mainstream beliefs about the census—gathered from news reports, Internet discussion forums, and websites in 2010—included:

- Worries that the government would collect DNA from the saliva of the person licking and sealing the census envelope.
- That GPS-location data gathered about U.S. households could be used for a future oppressive government action.

The Knowledge Gap

Americans may be obsessed with knowledge, but that doesn't mean they all have their facts straight. From trivia board games to *Jeopardy!* to spelling bees and online quizzes, many people seem eager to test their knowledge. And with more than 2,000 colleges, 20,000 public high schools, and widespread access to the Internet in the United States, you'd think people would share a set of basic information.

More than 13 million Americans have master's degrees, and more than 5 million others own doctoral or professional degrees. But despite all those diplomas, and even though they live in the Information Age, some Americans have knowledge gaps that range from comical to downright scary.

Common Core, an education research group, gave 17-year-olds a grade of "D" on the group's 2008 quiz on U.S. history. Half of those surveyed didn't know when the Civil War happened or what the Renaissance was. More than a fourth of young Americans participating in the survey thought that Columbus sailed the ocean blue not in 1492, but sometime after 1750. That doesn't even rhyme!

History Knowledge by 17-Year-Olds

43% Think the American Civil War happened before 1850 or after 1900

20% Can't identify the enemies of the U.S. during World War II

23% Can't identify Adolf Hitler

33% Don't know that the Bill of Rights covers freedom of speech and religion

Source: Common Core

I Could Make It in New York, if I Just Knew Where It Was

When it comes to geography, you might be better off trusting a GPS device over a young friend's driving directions. The most recent National Geographic and Roper survey of 18- to 24-year-old Americans, conducted in 2006, found that half couldn't find New York or Ohio on a map. And even right after Hurricane Katrina devastated the Gulf Coast and sparked nonstop news coverage for months, a significant number of young adults couldn't find Louisiana (33%) or Mississippi (48%) on the map, either.

Unless they get to "ask the audience" or "phone a friend," as was allowed on the TV show *Who Wants to Be a Millionaire?,* young adults were even more iffy on world geography and culture, the survey found. Fewer than half could find Iraq on a world map, despite the lengthy war fought by Americans in that country during the past decade. A whopping 88 percent couldn't locate Afghanistan, either. Sudan? Twenty percent thought the African nation was somewhere in Asia; 10 percent placed Sudan in Europe. Nearly half of young Americans said Islam, not Hinduism, is the majority religion in India.

The National Geographic study found that three-fourths of young Americans are sure that English has more native speakers than any other language on Earth. Confidence is good, but the correct answer is Mandarin Chinese.

You Don't Know Squat Either, Grandpa

Before people in older generations get too smug about how much kids these days don't know, consider this: A 2009 survey of civic literacy by the Intercollegiate Studies Institute showed little difference in average knowledge by Americans from all age groups, incomes, and political affiliations.

Fewer than half of Americans could name all three branches of the government, ISI discovered. A paltry 21% recognized Abraham Lincoln's Gettysburg Address as the source of the phrase "of the people, by the people, for the people." And only slightly more than that, 27%, knew that the Bill of Rights in the U.S. Constitution bans the establishment of an official religion for the country.

The nonprofit Marist Institute for Public Opinion discovered in 2010 that about a quarter of Americans don't know that their country won its independence from Great Britain. Six percent of people guessed France, China, Japan, Mexico, or Spain, while another 20 percent just weren't sure.

The legal information website Findlaw.com reported in mid-2010 that two-thirds of American adults it surveyed were unable to name a single current justice of the U.S. Supreme Court. A few show-offs—just 1 percent—were able to name all nine justices at the time of the survey.

Yeah, But We Know Science, Right?

Americans' knowledge of selected science facts:

- 53% Know how long it takes the Earth to revolve around the sun
- 59% Know that dinosaurs and early humans didn't live at the same time
- 47% Can estimate how much of the Earth's surface is covered with water

Source: California Academy of Sciences survey by Harris Interactive (2009)

Historical Amnesia

The scholarly American Revolution Center, which has been collecting historical objects for more than a century, surveyed more than 1,000 adults in the United States in mid-2009 and found that:

- More Americans knew that Michael Jackson sang "Beat It" than knew that the Bill of Rights is part of the U.S. Constitution.
- Sixty percent of Americans knew there were eight children in the household of reality-TV show couple Jon and Kate Gosselin, but more than one-third didn't know that the American Revolution happened in the 18th century.
- Half of those surveyed thought the Revolution happened after the Civil War and the War of 1812.
- A third mistakenly believed that the Bill of Rights does not guarantee a right to a trial by jury, while 40 percent wrongly believed that it secured the right to vote.
- More than half misidentified the American system of government as a direct democracy, rather than a republic.

Fortunately, the survey revealed that more than 90 percent of Americans think the history and principles of the American Revolution should be taught in schools. Good idea.

American Brain Power

Relax. There's no test at the end of this chapter. That should be a relief to those Americans who feel overwhelmed by the endless ways society measures people's intelligence, memory, brain functions, and learning styles. On the other hand, it may be a disappointment to the millions of Americans who seem compelled to test themselves. They volunteer for all manner of informal knowledge testing, from completing crossword and sudoku puzzles to guessing out loud while watching *Jeopardy!*

The Dreaded Entrance Exams

Two acronyms haunt the dreams of college-bound students: SAT and ACT. Each standardized college entrance exam is taken by more than a million American students each year. Test strategies, preparation books, and classes abound. Most young people do the best they can, submit less-than-perfect scores to their target colleges, and hope that the admissions office will consider their other qualifications, too.

But every year, a relative handful of students achieve perfect scores on the SAT or ACT. In 2010, 588 Americans scored a perfect 36 on the ACT—out of the 1.4 million who participated. That's more than twice as many perfect ACT scores than in 2006. In 2010, the College Board reported that 297 of 1.5 million students scored a perfect 2400 on the SAT.

Feats and Foes of Mind and Memory

Long before college entrance exams, many young Americans have their brainpower assessed through an IQ test. Although intelligence tests vary, most are designed to measure a person's mental ability compared to other people and predict how well the person may perform in school or at a job. The "average" person's IQ is generally said to be around 100.

Mensa, a voluntary organization for people with IQs of at least 132, claims 50,000 American members. A few other organizations have even higher IQ standards for membership. The Prometheus Society (164) and Mega Society (176) are two of the brainiest.

Noted American Mensans

- Geena Davis, actress
- Donald Petersen, former chairman of Ford Motor Company
- Adrian Cronauer, radio host, subject of *Good Morning, Vietnam*
- Marilyn Vos Savant, *Parade* columnist, owner of the world's highest recorded IQ (228)

Source: Mensa

Those of us who are glad if we can just remember where we left our car keys can only admire the memory skills of participants in the annual USA Memory Championship. Participants compete in a series of events such as memorizing a sequence of 100 single numbers, a 50-line free-verse poem, the order of multiple decks of cards, and the names and photographs of 99 people.

On the other extreme, more than 5 million Americans are afflicted with Alzheimer's disease, according to the Alzheimer's Association. The condition kills brain cells and can cause memory loss, dementia, and other serious problems. Alzheimer's disease is the seventh-leading cause of death in the nation.

Learning Disabilities

For some Americans, learning doesn't come easily. An unknown number of children and adults have learning disabilities in reading, writing, math, communication, or behavior. According to the National Center for Learning Disabilities, 2.6 million students have been diagnosed with LD and are in a special education program in American schools.

Learning Disability Facts

- Nearly half of learning disabled high school students perform three or more grade levels below their enrolled grade.
- Sixty-one percent of LD students receive high school diplomas compared to 87.6% of students overall.
- A quarter of students with LD drop out of high school, compared to less than 10% of all students.

Source: National Center for Learning Disabilities

Synesthesia

Synesthesia is a rare brain condition that causes a person to experience senses in unusual ways. For example, a synesthete may "hear" music or see written words or numbers as colors. What most people think of as a smell could be perceived by a synesthete as shapes. Hearing the word *red* could cause a taste sensation in the mouth.

It's unknown how many people actually have synesthesia, in part because those who have it may keep quiet about it to avoid potential ridicule or unwanted attention. Estimates of the synesthete population vary widely. Scottish psychologists published research in 2008 in the neurology journal *Brain* in which they calculated that there are 930,000 American children with a mild form of synesthesia. Other experts, such as Richard E. Cytowic, neurologist and author of *The Man Who Tasted Shapes,* put the number of actual synesthetes at 10 in every million humans, or about 3,000 Americans.

People with this condition are statistically more likely to be female and, according to some studies, more often are left-handed. Synesthetes often pass along the condition genetically to their children.

Some major artists and composers in history, such as Vincent van Gogh and Ludwig von Beethoven, are believed by some historians to have had the condition. Other art and music historians counter that these and other creative figures only used unconventional sensory terms to describe their art. But whether or not they actually heard colorful notes or painted musical colors, some "synesthetic" American artists continue to stretch people's thinking about what it means to hear, see, touch, smell, and feel.

Famous American Synesthetes

- Leonard Bernstein, composer and conductor
- Duke Ellington, jazz composer and bandleader
- Jimi Hendrix, rock guitarist
- John Mayer, blues guitarist
- Edgar Allan Poe, author
- Nikola Tesla, inventor and electrical engineer

Source: Incorrect Pleasures, an Internet blog authored by Australian synesthete Lil Marlene

Americans and Their Faith

Ministers lament the empty seats they see in their churches, but studies show that America still has broad and deep religious ties. A Gallup survey revealed that more than 43% of Americans say they attend church, synagogue, or mosque weekly or several times a month. And Pew found that more than 83% of adults say they are affiliated with a specific faith.

The Pew Forum on Religion & Public Life surveyed more than 35,000 Americans and found these self-professed affiliations:

1.	Protestant	51.3%
2.	Catholic	23.9%
3.	Nothing in particular	12.1%
4.	Agnostic	2.4%
5.	Mormon	1.7%
6.	Jewish	1.7%
7.	Atheist	1.6%
8.	Other faiths and world religions	1.5%

9. Don't know or refused 0.8%
10. Buddhist 0.7%
11. Jehovah's Witness 0.7%
12. Orthodox Christian (various) 0.6%
13. Muslim (various) 0.6%
14. Hindu 0.4%

To fully understand the spiritual trends, you have to look inside the numbers. More than one-fourth of adults are no longer part of the religious tradition in which they were raised. And a quarter of young Americans (18 to 29) have no religious affiliation.

By the time Pew conducts another survey, fewer than half of Americans may be Protestant—which would be a first for this country. But the decline in Catholic affiliation is more rapid: Some 24% of adults say they are Catholic, yet nearly one-third were raised in that faith. The face of American Catholicism continues to reflect immigration trends. Just as earlier surges in Irish and Italian immigration boosted the ranks of U.S. Catholics, Latinos now comprise one-third of Catholics—and nearly half of Catholics age 18 to 29.

Top 5 and Bottom 5 Churchgoing U.S. States in 2010

1. Mississippi 63%
2. Alabama 58%
3. South Carolina 56%
4. Louisiana 56%
5. Utah 56%
46. Nevada 30%
47. Massachusetts 29%
48. Maine 27%
49. New Hampshire 26%
50. Vermont 23%

Percent refers to near-weekly attendance. Source: Gallup.

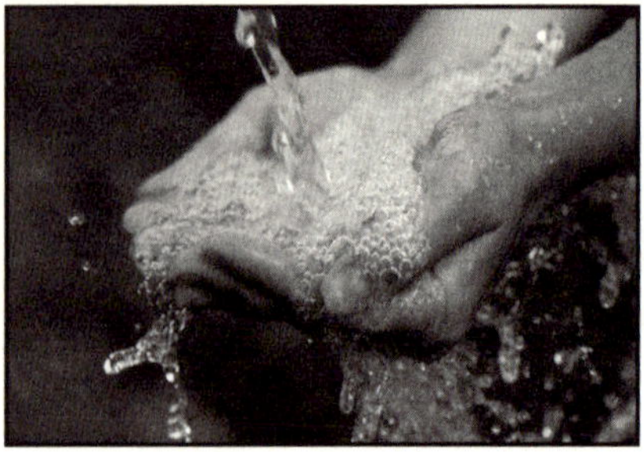

What Surveys Say About Us

It's hard to get through a day in America without encountering some attempt to measure people's opinions. It could be the latest published approval numbers on Congress, a quick survey that pops up when you visit an Internet site, a phone call from a nonpartisan research firm that interrupts your dinner, or the "Honk if you love (YOUR CAUSE HERE)" bumper sticker on that car in front of you.

The nightly news, weekly political shows, and mainstream Internet networks focus mostly on polls about politics and the economy, or on skepticism about climate change or immigration policy. But those results hardly scratch the surface of what Americans tell total strangers every day in polls.

Here's a random sample of what polls say Americans think:

Taxing junk food won't work. Asked by a CBS News poll whether putting a special tax on junk food would cause people to lose weight, 26% said yes but 72% said no way. The other 2% were either unsure or were stuffing their face with Cheetos when the pollster called.

A majority of men claim they won't date women who litter. A Timberland Company survey of American men found that 54% claimed they would have doubts about whether to date a woman who litters. One-fourth of those surveyed said they weren't sure if they'd go out with a woman who didn't recycle, either. This could be a sign that environmentalism is gaining ground. Or maybe some guys just have a new explanation: No, that cute girl didn't turn me down for a date; I just lost interest when she threw that Pepsi can in the trash.

People are washing their hands more often (and creepy researchers are watching). A study by scientific observers in public restrooms found recently that 85% of people wash their hands in the sink after using the toilet. A telephone poll during the same study, which was sponsored by the American Society for Microbiology and the American Cleaning Institute, found that 96% of people claim they wash their hands in public restrooms. Sounds like 11% aren't coming clean.

Americans think it's better to be rich than thin, young, or smart. A Harris poll in 2010 found that, if given a choice, more Americans would choose to be richer (43%) if the other choices were younger, smarter, or thinner. In the same poll, more than twice as many women (29%) than men (14%) picked being thinner as their preference.

We are suckers for "Made in America." Another Harris poll revealed that nearly two-thirds of Americans are more likely to buy a product that claims to be "Made in America." The poll didn't include any information about how many of those participants drive imported cars, drink German beer, or were answering the survey on a telephone or computer made in China.

Americans have more confidence in soldiers than senators. It's not all that surprising that in Gallup's July 2010 survey of attitudes toward 16 key American institutions, the military ranked first and Congress ranked last. In fact, the military has been first or second in the confidence survey every year since Gallup first asked the question in 1975. The full rankings show that both big business and organized labor don't get much love from the public, while small businesses and the police are generally held in high regard.

American Confidence in Institutions

Institution	Confidence
1. Military	76%
2. Small business	66%
3. Police	59%
4. Church/organized religion	48%
5. Medical system	40%
6. U.S. Supreme Court	36%
7. Presidency	36%
8. Public schools	34%
9. Criminal justice system	27%
10. Newspapers	25%
11. Banks	23%
12. Television news	22%
13. Organized labor	20%
14. Big business	19%
15. HMOs	19%
16. Congress	11%

Source: Gallup. Note: Confidence percentage combines "a great deal" and "a lot" answers.

Americans trust themselves more than they trust politicians. A September 2010 Gallup survey found that 69% of people have trust and confidence in the American people, but only 47% have the same level of trust and confidence in people holding or seeking political office.

American singles aren't looking for someone with a good personality. FastLife, a speed dating service, polled 1,000 single American men and women and found that 42% of women and 58% of men put high importance on physical beauty in potential partners. Women were most likely to prefer men with brown or black hair, while men were slightly more interested in brunettes than blondes. Both men and women said they favor blue eyes. But among those willing to say where they are looking other than a person's face, women rated a man's stomach the most important feature. Men rated the female derriere first.

Fatherhood matters. In an era when many American children receive plenty of good parenting from shared custody arrangements or other nontraditional family settings, a survey by the National Fatherhood Initiative found that eight of 10 American fathers agree that a man does a better job as a parent if he is married to the mother of their child.

Some people would try brain-implant Internet access. A quirky Zogby survey of thousands of Internet users in 2007 asked how likely Americans would be to accept a brain-implanted device for use in accessing the Internet. A surprising 11% of people said they were very likely, or somewhat likely, to do so. The same poll found that 18% of people would be okay with using an implanted device in their own children to keep track of the kids' whereabouts.

U.S. Against the World

Americans are obsessed with measuring things, from test scores and incomes to height and weight. Many Americans are also fond of chanting with pride "We're number one!" or "U-S-A!" in international sports competitions such as the Olympics. But when it comes to comparisons with other nations in areas other than sports, it can be good or not so good to be at or near the top ranking. Either way, it's usually eye-opening.

NationMaster.com ranks nations of the world across a wide array of statistics using United Nations, Central Intelligence Agency, and other official sources of data. Although the self-reported nature of some of the information can cause distortions in rankings for some categories, it's fairly easy to see where the U.S. stands in categories such as economy, health, and education.

Where the U.S. Stands

With approximately 310 million people, the United States has the third largest population among nations of the world, according to the *CIA*

World Factbook. But there's little chance we'll ever catch up with No. 1 China, which has more than 1.3 billion people, or No. 2 India, with 1.1 billion. Indonesia (240 million) and Brazil (199 million) trail the U.S. in the rest of the top five.

That's because the U.S. ranks 154th in the world for birth rate, with just 13.83 births per year for every 1,000 people in the country. African nations lead the birth rate rankings. Niger, with a 51.6 birth rate, tops the list, followed by Uganda and Mali, each with birth rates in the mid-40s.

For some other developed nations, the birth rate has dropped so low that the countries are experiencing population declines. Hong Kong, with 7.42 births per 1,000 people, is last among 223 countries included in the birth rate rankings. Japan, Italy, and Germany round out the bottom four nations for birth rate.

Once an American is born, he or she can expect to live an average of 78 years, according to the *CIA World Factbook.* That's pretty good, but we're just youngsters in the life expectancy rankings. America ranks 49th among world nations. Leading the way is tiny Macau (84.36 years), an island Chinese territory that also happens to be one of the most densely populated places on the planet. Whatever people are eating there, everyone else should probably be taking notes.

Life Expectancy by Nation

Nation	Life Expectancy
1. Macau	84.36 years
2. Andorra	82.51
3. Japan	82.12
4. Singapore	81.98
5. Hong Kong	81.86
49. United States	78.11

Source: NationMaster.com

Of course, population size or growth rarely equates to individual economic success. In the latest estimates, the U.S. ranks 11th in Gross Domestic Product per capita, at $46,000. Nations with comparatively small populations dominate the GDP rankings.

Country	GDP per Capita
1. Liechtenstein	$ 122,100
2. Qatar	$ 119,500
3. Luxembourg	$ 79,600
4. Bermuda	$ 69,900
5. Norway	$ 57,400
11. United States	$ 46,000

Table Time Comparisons

When it comes to time spent eating, Americans give new meaning to the phrase "fast food," according to a *USA Today* analysis of a survey of member nations by the Organization for Economic Cooperation and Development (OECD). Americans, they say, spend about an hour and 15 minutes eating each day. North Americans in general eat fast. Only people in Mexico (66 minutes) and Canada (69 minutes) eat faster than Americans among OECD nations. The French, on the other extreme, claim to spend more than two hours a day eating and drinking, twice as much as their North American friends.

Top 5 and Bottom 5 Rankings

To get a sense of how the U.S. compares to the rest of the world, look at where the country leads the way—and where it brings up the rear.

For example, according to NationMaster's accumulated data, the United States has the dubious first-place ranking in total crimes per capita, divorce rate, obesity, and emissions of CO_2 per capita. On the other hand, we're tops in several positive categories, including total Gross Domestic Product and average education level of adults.

Not surprisingly, since the modern fast food restaurant chain is an American invention, we have by far the most McDonald's restaurants, at more than 12,000, trailed by Japan, Canada, and the United Kingdom. Last place in the McDonald's ranking goes to Iceland, which has just one set of golden arches.

Among categories in which the U.S. ranks second, some are not so desirable—reported murders and robberies—while others are signs of prosperity. Americans own more than 210 million televisions, meaning just about two TVs for every three people in the country. With so many cable TV and other programming options, however, that probably means that two of those people are fighting over who gets to hold the remote control. China is the hands-down leader in TV sets, with 400 million, and that number is expected to grow rapidly in coming years.

Critics of some worldwide rankings argue that democracies with free presses are more likely to report negative statistics, such as crimes, accurately. On the other hand, they say, closed societies or those led by authoritarian regimes may provide positive statistics on education, literacy, infant mortality, and other issues that cannot be independently verified.

When it comes to marijuana use, Americans (12%) trail only New Zealand (22%) and Australia (18%) in the percentage of people who say they have used cannabis. (The Aussies and Kiwis are taking their regional rivalry to a new high, you might say!) Another third-place ranking for the U.S. is total number of armed forces personnel, according to the International Institute for Strategic Studies. China and Russia lead the way. And despite the stereotype of oil-rich nations as being strictly Middle Eastern, the U.S. ranked third in 2007 in daily oil production.

Top-Ranked Nations for Barrels of Oil Produced Daily

1.	Saudi Arabia	10.2 million
2.	Russia	9.9 million
3.	United States	8.5 million

4.	Iran	4 million
5.	China	3.7 million
6.	Mexico	3.5 million
7.	Canada	3.4 million
8.	UAE	2.9 million

Source: CIA World Factbook

The U.S. ranks fourth in land area, drug offenses, the average size of houses, and number of days off work. We're fifth in executions per capita, teacher salaries, and income taxation.

Being in last place doesn't always sit well with Americans. But in some categories, it's not a bad thing to bring up the rear. The U.S. has the lowest rate of software piracy in the world, for instance, with one of every five software installations considered illegal. On the other end of the spectrum, Armenia, Moldova, Azerbaijan, Bangladesh, and Zimbabwe take piracy to extremes, with more than 90% of all software believed to be illegally obtained.

When it comes to drinking wine, Americans are last among 18 nations studied by Euromonitor for annual wine consumption per person. Americans drink what sounds like a respectable seven liters of wine a year, per person. But that is practically a dry country compared to the top three wine-drinking nations: Italy (54 liters), France (47), and Switzerland (42). Even the Swedes drink twice as much wine (16 liters a year per person) as Americans do.

Internet usage

China has the highest number of Internet users among nations of the world, with more people going online there (420 million) than the entire population of the United States. As a percentage of population, the U.S. is fifth, with its 240 million Internet users accounting for nearly 78% of the population.

Nation	Total Internet Users
1. China	420 million
2. United States	240 million
3. Japan	127 million
4. India	81 million
5. Brazil	76 million

Nation	Percentage Using Internet
1. United Kingdom	82%
2. South Korea	81%
3. Germany	79%
4. Japan	78%
5. United States	77%

Sources: Nielsen Online, International Telecommunications Union

Motor Vehicles

Americans definitely have the most cars. According to NationMaster.com, the U.S. has approximately 765 motor vehicles for every 1,000 people. Some days, it seems like all of them are on the highway at the same time.

Motor Vehicles per 1,000 People

Nation	Vehicles
1. United States	765
2. Luxembourg	686
3. Malaysia	641
4. Australia	619
5. Malta	607

The Unofficial U.S. Census at a Glance

Answers to 10 Questions the Official Census Neglected to Ask

1. What percent of Americans have at least one tattoo? *15% of Americans.*

2. What is the No. 1 reason for traveling? *To visit friends and relatives.*

3. What destination do more Americans travel to than any other in the U.S.? *Times Square, New York City.*

4. What percent of American pet owners say their pet is a better listener than their spouse? *25%.*

5. How much does the average American family spend per child on back-to-school clothing, shoes, and school supplies and equipment? *Over $600.*

6. Are more people eating donuts for breakfast now? *No. Only one in 10 Americans (10%) join Homer Simpson on a donut run for breakfast, compared to 17% in 1989.*

7. How big of a tip does the average person leave in a restaurant? *18%.*

8. How many of us go dancing at least two times a month? *3 million.*

9. Who reads more books—modern Americans or their counterparts in the 1950s? *Twice as many people read books now as compared to 1957.*

10. Which five states have the highest rates of participation in volunteer activities? *Utah followed by Iowa, Minnesota, Nebraska, and Alaska.*

All About Love, Sex, and Family

1. How much money do Americans spend each year on online dating services? *$1 billion.*

2. What percent of people say they are heterosexual? *97%.*

3. How often does the average American have sex? *118 times a year.*

4. How many families are one-parent households? *13 million.*

5. How many Americans live in a household that includes at least two adult generations? *16%.*

6. What percent of marriages of at least 10 years end in divorce? *25%.*

7. How many married people have a spouse from a different race or ethnicity? *14.6%.*

8. What day of the week is most popular for people to look at pornographic websites? *Sunday.*

9. Do you live alone? *10% of Americans say yes.*

10. If you are a single adult, are you looking for a relationship? *Only 17% say yes.*

What Americans Earn, Learn, and Give

1. Are you now enrolled in a school of any type? *26% of Americans say yes.*

2. For those of you with credit card debt, what's your average total card balance? *$15,788.*

3. Do you have a J-O-B? *45% of all Americans 16 and older are employed—the other half are students or retirees or are not working for other reasons.*

4. How many people 18 and older have a cell phone? *85%.*

5. What percent of people own at least one firearm? *23%.*

6. What percent of workers participate in a 401(k) or similar retirement savings plans at work? *45%.*

7. How long do you spend in the car every day? *The average is 55 minutes.*

8. What percent of Americans leave the house for work between midnight and 6 A.M.? *6%.*

9. How much does the average person donate to charity in a year? *Nearly $1,000.*

10. Did you give more to charity in 2009 than Stanley Druckenmiller, CEO at Duquesne Capital? *No. But no one in the country could say yes to that question, since Stanley and his wife gave more than $700 million through his family foundation.*

Americans' Digital Habits

1. Do you have high-speed Internet access at home? *60% of Americans can surf at broadband speeds.*
2. Are you on Facebook? *43% of Americans and counting have a Facebook page.*
3. Do you use the Internet for online banking? *26% of Americans say yes.*
4. What's the No. 1 how-to advice Americans search for on the Internet? *How to kiss.*
5. What percent of Americans use only a landline phone or only a cell phone for their home phone? *20% of those homes use a cell phone only, compared to just 17% still using only a traditional phone line.*
6. How many people still use a pay phone booth to make calls? *Nobody knows, but they place 1.7 billion calls a year.*
7. How old is the average video game player? *34.*
8. Where is the No. 1 U.S. state for jobs in the video game industry? *California.*
9. How many text messages do Americans send or receive? *1.5 trillion a year.*
10. Do you use the Internet to read news? *43% of Internet users say yes.*

Key Facts on How Americans Live and Die

1. How tall are you? *The average American adult male is 5'9" and the average woman is 5'4".*

2. Do you have a cardiovascular disease? *26% of Americans do.*

3. How many people have Alzheimer's disease? *More than 5 million Americans.*

4. Do you have arthritis? *22% of adults say they have some form of the condition.*

5. How much chicken does the average American eat? *60 pounds a year.*

6. Do you like ice cream? *Apparently. The average person eats 14 pounds of ice cream a year.*

7. Are you a vegetarian? *3% of Americans follow some type of vegetarian diet.*

8. How much sleep do Americans get? *Just 6.7 hours on weeknights.*

9. What's the likelihood that you will die from an encounter with a snake or other reptile? *One in 3.8 million.*

10. What's the most likely cause of death for an American? *Heart disease.*

Q&A on Crime and Punishment

1. Of all Americans arrested every year, what percent are male? *75%.*
2. How many people are in jail or prison or on probation or parole? *3% of American adults.*
3. What percent of children 17 and younger think lying and cheating is essential for success? *51%.*
4. How many high school students have cheated on tests? 75%.
5. How many Americans 12 and older use marijuana? *16 million.*
6. How much do Americans spend every year on prescription drugs? *$230 billion.*
7. Do you smoke or chew? *70 million Americans 12 and older use some form of tobacco regularly.*
8. Have you ever lied or cheated? *39% of people claim they never have.*
9. Do you drink alcohol? *42% of Americans say yes.*
10. What percent of married Americans have cheated with another sexual partner? *Between 10% and 33%.*

What's on the American Mind

1. Do you believe extraterrestrials have visited Earth? *24% of Americans believe they have.*

2. What percent of people believe the living can communicate with the dead? *21%.*

3. Do you have social anxiety disorder? *7% of Americans have a form of the condition.*

4. What percent of Americans who take the SAT get a perfect score? *One out of every 5,000 who take the test, or two one-hundredths of 1%!*

5. How many people go to a church, synagogue, or mosque weekly or several times a month? *43% of Americans.*

6. Would you be willing to have a brain-implanted device that would let you access the Internet? *11% of people said okay.*

7. Do you think the history and principles of the American Revolution should be taught in schools? *90% of Americans say yes.*

8. What percent of Americans know that dinosaurs and early humans didn't live at the same time. *59%.*

9. How many 17-year-olds can't name any of the enemies of the U.S. during World War II? *20%.*

10. How many people think the census is very important? *60% of Americans say the official census is very important, but 100% of smart, good-looking, popular people think this unofficial census is important enough to read!*